I0160955

I AM
Caroline

LOVE'S
DIVINE MESSENGER

Author ... Speaker ... Healer ... Teacher
Minister ... Psychic

IT'S TIME TO
Quickly ... Easily ... Painlessly
RELEASE THE
Fear ... Pain ... Anger
That No Longer Serves You

SO YOU CAN
Remember and Celebrate Your Magnificent Divine Self
LET ME SHOW YOU HOW!

Start by doing what's necessary;
then do what's possible;
and suddenly
you are doing the impossible.

~ Francis of Assisi ~
https://www.biography.com/people/st-francis-of-assisi-21152679#!

WHAT WOULD LOVE DO?

The Magical Question

That Gives You

The Perfect Answer

Every Time!

By
Caroline McIntosh

LOVE'S DIVINE MESSENGER

I saw that you were perfect
and so I loved you.

Then I saw that you were not perfect
and I loved you more.

~ Unknown ~

CHAPTERS OF YOUR LIFE

Chapter 1

I walk down the street.
There is a deep hole in the sidewalk
I fall in. I am lost. I am hopeless. It isn't my fault.
It takes forever to find a way out.

Chapter 2
I walk down the same street.
There is a deep hole in the sidewalk.
I pretend I don't see it. I fall in again.
I can't believe I'm in the same place.
But it isn't my fault.
It still takes a long time to get out.

Chapter 3
I walk down the same street.
There is a deep hole in the sidewalk.
I see it is there. I still fall in ... it's a habit.
My eyes are open; I know where I am;
It is my fault. I get out immediately.

Chapter 4
I walk down the same street.
There is a deep hole in the sidewalk.
I walk around it.

Chapter 5
I walk down another street.

~ Portia Nelson ~
There's a Hole in My Sidewalk: The Romance of Self-Discovery
http://www.masterworksbroadway.com/artist/portia-nelson-0/

What chapter are you living?

Asking the Magical Question
will always lead you down the other street.

Don't should on me
and
I won't should on you!

~ I Am Caroline ~
www.IAmCaroline.com

PRAISE FOR
The Magical Question - What Would LOVE Do?

Great Book!
This book lovingly reminds us that
we have a choice in every moment.
Choose LOVE. Choose this Book.

~ DR. JOE VITALE ~
Star of the Movie
THE SECRET and 15 OTHER MOVIES
Author of over 50 books to mention, including the bestsellers
THE ATTRACTOR FACTOR, ZER0 LIMITS
and latest THE AWAKENED MILLIONAIRE

VISIT
http://www.MrFire.com

~ JOHN HARRICHARAN ~
Caroline's book,
WHAT WOULD LOVE DO?
is an amazing collection of stories
that show the true power of LOVE.
As you read page after page, you will find
that your soul starts to sing.
These heart-warming stories show you that
each and everyone has the ability to transform
lives using the awesome power of LOVE.
Award-winning author of the bestseller
WHEN YOU CAN WALK ON WATER ... TAKE THE BOAT

VISIT
www.insight2000.com AND http://johnharricharan-consultations.com/

I'm speechless!
This book is what the world needs ... now!
Inspiring, heart-warming, soul-moving ...
it's beautiful, in pure excellence!
Caroline gently reaches in and turns on the
light of your heart. Get this book and learn to
ask the Magical Question and watch
as your life changes.

~ BRYAN HALL ~
Live Success Coach, Author, Spiritual Electrician, Motivational Expert

VISIT
www.spiritualnetworks.com/bryanhall/

Using Dr. David Hawkin's book
POWER VS FORCE – THE MAP of CONSCIOUSNESS
I measured
WHAT WOULD LOVE DO?
for its level of consciousness
and found it to be at the
Level of Enlightenment 700-1000
I highly recommend Caroline's book
for everyone!

~ HELENE MONTPELLIER ~
Chelmsford, Ontario, Canada

VISIT
www.CoCreationsUnlimited.com/truth/consciousness.html
TO LEARN MORE

PUBLISHED BY

LOVE'S OPEN HOUSE PUBLISHING CO.
94 Alma, Hanmer, Ontario, Canada, P3P 1R2

LET'S TALK ... 1-705-831-2022

EMAIL .... Love@IAmCaroline.com

WhatWouldLoveDo@eastlink.ca

SKYPE Loves1stCaroline

WEBSITE .... www.IAmCaroline.com

www.WhatWouldLoveDo.online

Data - McIntosh, Caroline, Inspirational, Motivational, Healing, Spiritual, Psychic, Suicide, Death, Counseling, Children, Pink Ribbon, Self Esteem, Self-Help, Soul's Purpose

Revised Edition E-Book ISBN 978-0-9783508-4-0

First Edition - ISBN 1-4140-6272-9

Second Edition – ISBN 978-1-897564-18-9

This book and other products created at LOH (LOVE's Open House) is part of an affiliate program.

To become an affiliate contact Caroline at LOVE'S OPEN HOUSE PUBLISHING address above.

Do not pray for an easy life,
pray for the strength
to endure a difficult one.

~ Bruce Lee ~
http://www.imdb.com/name/nm0000045/bio

TABLE OF CONTENTS

It is never too late to be
what you might have been.

~ George Eliot ~
http://www.notablebiographies.com/Du-Fi/Eliot-George.html

DEDICATION

This book is dedicated to
YOU!

I cannot do what I have come to do
WITHOUT YOU!

WE NEED EACH OTHER

JOIN ME IN THE

LOVE VOLUTION™

www.LoveVolution.ca

A grass roots movement
About to set the world on fire with the
Sacred, spiritual, flame burning inside you now.
By always asking
THE MAGICAL QUESTION

Play a vital part …
Become a Spiritual Electrician.
Reach into people's hearts and turn their light on.

Asking

THE MAGICAL QUESTION … WHAT WOULD LOVE DO?

Will show you how.

Great minds discuss ideas.
Average minds discuss events.
Small minds discuss people.

~ Eleanor Roosevelt ~
https://www2.gwu.edu/~erpapers/abouteleanor/erbiography.cfm

ACKNOWLEDGMENTS

At the end of October 2003, I asked the universe to send me a mentor who could show me how to market and fund my not-for-profit club, The G.O.D. S.Q.U.A.D. Serving Communities, Inc. (outlined in chapter - LOVE's Club).

That same day a stranger's email asked, "Do you have what it takes to be an enlightened millionaire?" I filled out the questionnaire and qualified to join Mark Victor Hansen's (co-author of Chicken Soup for the Soul) and Robert Allen's Enlightened Millionaire program.

I quickly realized this program would not serve my needs. It was suggested I enter Robert Allen's mentoring program. The Canadian exchange rate made the cost more than my credit card could handle so I went within and asked, *What would LOVE do?* and heard, *Talk it over with John.*

My sweetheart John, offered to fund my dream if I promised to give it my all; however, if my efforts didn't produce financial success I would have to go out and get a 'real' job. I thank John for making this possible. I think he is beginning to realize this IS my real job.

Three days after asking the universe for help, my mentor Greg McKeown phoned me. I should thank him for his contagious enthusiasm, for believing in my dream and for coming up with the most logical, appropriate next step in my life.

As I shared the other ideas I was bursting with, wise Greg knew I needed an umbrella for all my projects.

When I told him the club's motto he exploded, "That's it!" and the What Would LOVE Do? Foundation was conceived with the G.O.D. S.Q.U.A.D. as its main focus.

Thirty or more years of asking The Magical Question (TMQ) provided the stories in this book. I needed a graphic artist with book experience to design the cover. I knew no one. Again, I asked TMQ.

LOVE knew I didn't have the money necessary so, it made me think of a young man who had offered his help in the past.

Tons of thanks must go out to the team of Bob Stevens and Chris Evans of Add Experience. They created the wonderful cover you hold in your hands, a cover that "feeds the heart and the soul" in exchange for helping a family member face a fear.

Money was needed to publish What Would LOVE Do? and when I asked TMQ I remembered a marketing idea that had helped others. I sent a draft copy of the cover with an email to people I knew and offered the book at a special pre-release price. My gratitude goes to the trusting souls who responded, all listed in my first edition.

Special and heartfelt thanks to the characters in the stories. They provided the food to feed, heal, and inspire the soul. Their names have been changed to respect their privacy, especially those of the children who continue to walk and talk the truth.

Jean Lafleur, Diana Holloway and Fern Rancourt are to be thanked for believing in TMQ and for sharing some of their experiences to show you how easy it is to do the same and even more.

I wish to acknowledge some of the wonderful teachers who have blessed my life, Sri Sathya Sai Baba, Tom Sawyer, His Holiness The Dalai Lama, Ram Dass, Marilyn Rosner, Olga Whorrell, Daniel Chesbro, Shirley MacLaine, Connie Newton, and Alberto Aguas.

I have had many teachers but these influenced me in a very specific and profound way. Someday I hope I can personally thank these earth angels who fed my soul in their unique way, Oprah Winfrey, Dr. David Suzuki, Nelson Mandela, Kathy Buckley, Bryan Hall, Greg McKeown, John Harricharan, Dr. "Patch" Adams, and Robert Allen.

I must thank all my invisible helpers, protectors, guides, teachers, inspirers, comforters, and prodders - who gave me exactly what I needed, when I needed it, in a way that was best for all concerned. Their names are too numerous to mention, and some I don't even know.

I believe we are spiritual entities having a human experience and LOVE always sends special angels to help us through our dark days. I am who I am today because of them.

Some specialized in trying to dim my light, forcing me shine brighter. Others fueled my flame by gently and lovingly fanning it.

Some loved so much they volunteered to be my Judas or persecutor. Some loved so much, they let me make my own mistakes. Then there were those whose souls loved and trusted me enough to allow me to be their Judas or angel.

Each and everyone one of you knows which role you played, and I humbly thank you for doing so.

Every single person I have met has become a page in my 'book of knowledge' and I am in indebted to you, until the end of time.

I wish to honor you by thanking you publicly for volunteering to play the role I needed.

- ♥ Mom and Dad, Jean and Ted Lafleur – (both deceased) who adopted me and supported me all the way;
- ♥ My siblings - Carl, Raymond, Susan, Larry, Monica, and Rose -each occupying a special place in my heart;
- ♥ My birth mother - thanks for giving me the gift of life, you did the right thing;
- ♥ Former husband and still great friend, John McIntosh and his new partner, Denise Butler;
- ♥ Johanne 'JohJoh' Abonader - who taught me how to go first class and so much more;
- ♥ Parveen Mecci - the perfect host, always grace and LOVE in action;
- ♥ JoAnna and Barry Dale for introducing me to Unity and Divine Order and for greatly helping finance my book;

- ♥ Audetti Talleck Knox - a tiny angelic dynamo and her son Joshua – both are definitely Earth Angels;
- ♥ Dr. Adrianne Ball for her dedication and sense of humor;
- ♥ Fern Rancourt - a superb artist, writer and networker;
- ♥ Cecile Coutu - a walking miracle;
- ♥ Lynn Simonato - who is becoming more fearless by the minute;
- ♥ Warren Schuteker - a modern day Moses;
- ♥ Laura Cotesta -17-year-old angel still inspiring us from the other side;
- ♥ Lyse Larocque-Laurin - who trusted LOVE enough to stop teaching and start living her dream;
- ♥ Toula Sakelaris - a most generous friend, volunteer and entrepreneur extraordinaire;
- ♥ My Kingston, Ontario, Canada lights, Marlene Fletcher, Alice Fletcher, Barb Greenshields, and others - for supplying the tissues and all the laughs.

There are special lights who make up part of my present dream team - Lise Beaulieu, my 'fun' friends Helene Montpelier, Dorothy Unruh, Jeannine Tasse, Lillian Rivet, and Louise Alexander.

A special thanks to you, dear reader for reading and sharing What Would LOVE Do? with others.

I invite you to become part of a grassroots movement that is about to give birth to a magnificent, noble, new way of being on planet Earth; filled with peace, joy, wonder, abundance, significance and in awe of humankind, the earth, and all of her creations.

I've been shown a glimpse of the future

and it is glorious!

Let's bring heaven down to Earth,

here and now.

IT IS TIME!

SHOULD YOU BUY THIS BOOK?

- ♥ Are you or your loved ones experiencing chaos in your life, at work, and in matters of the heart or your health?
- ♥ Are you spending a lot of time and money getting help the traditional way only to find out you still don't have peace and joy, or know your life's purpose, or your soul mate?
- ♥ Have you tried alternative solutions, hands-on healing, religion, counseling, workshops, crystals, psychics, spirituality and everything else out there?
- ♥ Or, are you one of the 'lucky ones' who seems to have the perfect life yet still feel like something's missing?

I am the humble author of this amazing and revealing book; I went through all the above and more! I was born asking, "Why?" for everything and I drove all my teachers crazy because they didn't always have the answers.

Unable to get satisfaction and to escape what seemed like mental torture, I became totally physical by joining the Canadian Air Force in 1967 as a Physical Education and Recreation Instructor.

Pushing myself physically suppressed my mental body, for a short period of time. However, the pull of the "Why?" did not die, it just became stronger.

Sixteen years later I left my physical, military life and completely immersed myself in an invisible, metaphysical world seeking the key that would unlock the door to all the answers.

I quickly exhausted the traditional methods and then certified in and practiced many alternative healing and counseling techniques, traveled the world, studied with the best, learned a great deal and taught all ages. Still, I hadn't found the key I intuitively knew was available for all. Upon returning from Egypt I had an awakening; I remembered! In order to always get the perfect answer, one had to ask the right question! It took me most of the day, praying and meditating to realize the 'right' question!

The magical question, what would LOVE do? simplified and empowered my life so much that miracles began manifesting through me and in the lives of those who began asking the same question. My mentor quickly realized I was inspired and determined to fulfill my destiny. He knew I needed an umbrella for all my projects, and when I told him my idea for a club and the motto, he knew we had hit the jackpot! The What Would LOVE Do? Foundation was conceived. This book would help fund it and my many other projects.

Just before printing, it was realized the legalities of a Foundation would limit LOVE's usage of funds raised so another inviting, inclusive, and easily remembered name was sought.

LOVE's OPEN HOUSE – LOH was it!

LOVE'S OPEN HOUSE
Your H.O.M.E. (Heaven On Mother Earth)
Away from HOME (Heaven)
Come to LOH to get HIGH on LIFE!

LOVE's OPEN HOUSE welcomes and supports all people, places and projects that recognize, nurture and protect the uniqueness and oneness of all.

I was inspired to donate $5 from the sale of each book to fund a new program for the homeless that would empower them to decide how the money would best serve them.

It is time on this planet for each to realize his or her full potential. It is time to move from success to significance.

Every single person on this planet is significant! Each of us makes a difference! The true stories in this book will inspire and empower you to do the same, and even more.

You will learn more about me, LOVE'S club and my mission to teach LOVE.

The children's stories will amaze you.

You will also see what happens when others start to ask that simple yet profound question, What would LOVE do?

Don't take my word for it. Try it for yourself. See how it can simply and quickly change every aspect of your life.

After you've had your own experience, you're invited to share it with others. Your story may be included in the next edition of What Would LOVE Do? We hope this is just the first of many to come.

Did you notice how the cover caught your eye and moved you to pick up this book, inviting you to begin your real work, to be LOVE in action, and to find out a key was never necessary.

The door was never locked!

You are here to serve LOVE and LOVE wants to serve you.

Still wondering if you should buy this book?

What would LOVE do?

LOVE'S MESSAGE TO YOU

I, LOVE, The Source, Universal Mind, The Life-Force, Creator, All that is, the God of your understanding, whatever name you feel most comfortable with, wish to give you a message. Let Me call Myself LOVE.

YOU are very important to Me, to the planet and to all of humanity. It is time to know that I love you exactly as you are at this moment, regardless of what you are feeling, thinking, saying, or doing to yourself or to others!

I express Myself through you every time you share your gifts, your LOVE, and your light. I ask that you be My ambassador, to represent Me, to be LOVE in action on this planet.

I have been moving through you and sending you messages all your life. The cells of your body were imprinted with all that you need to know before you were born! The clues are all around you; in the people and experiences you attract, in the song that won't stop playing over and over in your mind, on every sign that you read, and in every book that you pick up, especially this one.

Picking up this book signaled that you are ready to remember who you are and to begin your life's work. Your eyes, the windows to your soul, always record My messages. It is time to decode some of them so that you can better understand them and act accordingly.

Think of Me, LOVE, as your boss - the wisest, most powerful, prosperous forgiving, brave, generous, empowering, protective, and gentle boss in the universe who loves and knows you better than you can love or know yourself; and who always has your best interest at heart.

I want the best job done, in the most energy efficient way possible, by the most qualified person. I have carefully selected and groomed you for each and every assignment. Don't all wise bosses want their companies, employees, and partners to succeed?

For you to be successful, happy, healthy, and prosperous, simply decide who you want to work with - fear or Me?

We are the only ones who motivate humans to do what they do. If you analyze every action, you will soon realize the only fear that exists is ... the fear of not being loved!

If you choose to partner with Me, know I may ask you to do something you don't want to do or are afraid to do; however, when that happens, I will also give you all that you need to succeed - courage, desire, ability, time, money, patience, joy, opportunity - whatever is necessary!

What I enjoy most is watching you grow through your fears and anger; growing in your trust of Me and My ability to provide all that you need, want and more.

There will come a time when you joyfully, blindly step off the cliff to serve Me (like the fool in the tarot cards) because you know I will always be there to catch you.

Every act is a cry for LOVE. The uglier the deed, the greater the need. I want to answer that call; however, I need to move through you to do so because, I AM potential invisible energy, too powerful to be on Earth in full physical form. Let Me slow myself down and move through you, so that I can be physically manifested, solid, and known by all who are crying for Me, through you!

Our partnership will astound and amaze those who don't understand. They will ask how you can be so calm and fearless in the presence of something that would frighten the bravest.

When asked, go within and allow Me to speak through you, and together we will say exactly what each person needs to hear. Together we will show them that LOVE is the greatest power.

You and I are One. We cannot be divided, conquered, or lost. The choice is always yours. Remember, no matter what you choose, My LOVE for you never changes because to deny you is to deny Myself. Join Me. Be My ambassador, and let's have fun with it. Let us be 'Spiritual Electricians,' reaching into people's hearts to light their light on!

If you choose to gift this book to someone, be My messenger.

Simply ask, "What would LOVE write?" and fill in the blanks, on the YOUR MINI READING page with the first answers that come to your knowing.

Trusting Me will become so easy - second nature - just like breathing. When it does, be ready to have others be in awe of you. Simply remind them they can do the same as you, and even more.

Little giggles of delight explode inside Caroline/Me every time I think of your future because I know the joy it holds for you. Isn't this fun! Aren't you glad you bought this book?

YOUR MINI READING

Now, let's see what I want to tell you …

THE MAIN COLOR OF YOUR AURA IS …
(Colors explained on page 343)

_____

PAGE WITH A SPECIAL MESSAGE FOR YOU IS …

_____

YOUR GIFT TO HUMANITY IS …

_____

_____

_____

_____

_____

_____

_____

_____

_____

_____

YOUR MINI READING FOR OTHERS ...

I KNOW you can do this for others as well as I can.

You may contact Caroline for help if you feel the need. However, let's see what you come up with first.

TRUST in Me. Simply ask, "What would LOVE say it is?"

COLOR ... Close your eyes and ask, "What is the first color that comes to mind for this person?"

The first color that popped into your mind, that you heard, thought, felt, smelled or tasted is it. It's that simple! IF you get more than one color, which is the 1st one that popped into your knowing? That's the one you write.

PAGE NUMBER ... Do the same for the page number. What is the 1st number popped into your knowing? Write that.

GIFT TO HUMANITY ... This one may seem a tad harder at first; however, all you have to do is breathe and be willing to let LOVE, Me guide you.

Trust the first words, thoughts, feelings, knowings, that come into your mind as you ask, "What is so special or what stands out about this person that inspires others?"

Or you might be moved to look at the challenges in that person's life. Their gift may be the opposite of the troubles that surround them.

For example, if a person is here to demonstrate MY power of LOVE through forgiveness that person will automatically attract people who need forgiving.

So, forgiveness could be that person's gift to humanity!

What would LOVE write?

Allow yourself to be inspired. There are no mistakes. You will amaze yourself if you just ... TRUST!

A FUN WAY TO USE THIS BOOK ... OR ANY BOOK!

Think of a question you would like to have an answer to.

IF you have no question, simply ask, "What general message do You, LOVE, have for me today?"

Then, close your eyes, take a deep breath, relax and leaf through this book until you are moved to stop.

Then notice where your eyes go.

Was it the title, a line, a paragraph or are you moved to read the whole chapter?

Some don't see My answer clearly at first, however; after some time, they get it.

IF you truly do not get the answer, contact Caroline to help you.

Love is like the wind,
you can't see it, but you can feel it.

~ Nicholas Sparks ~
http://nicholassparks.com/about/

HELPFUL NOTES

- ♥ LOVE in upper case, capital letters, is used to differentiate it from love.
- ♥ LOVE is divine, perfect, detached, unconditional, expressed in every cell of your being, IS YOU!
- ♥ love is human, imperfect, emotional, conditional, attached to the ego.
- ♥ There are no such things as accidents. For example, you were destined to read this book.
- ♥ You had to pass three tests before this book called to you.
    1. You are in the middle of or about to make a major change in your life in regard to health, attitude, relationship, job, beliefs, location and so forth, and you need some direction.
    2. You have a great deal of personal power. You can change the energy of a room, in a positive or negative way, just by walking into it, without even saying a word.
    3. You are ready to begin your spiritual work, the real reason you came to Earth because, Caroline is a teacher of teachers. You are truly ready to begin your spiritual work.
- ♥ You may have picked What Would LOVE Do? for someone else. Who do you think of when holding this book? Share it with that person.
- ♥ At the spiritual level, everyone is absolute perfection, like a 1000-watt bulb, in the Creator's eyes. Some shine at 20 watts, some at 50, 100 or 500 watts.

- ♥ The dust on your light bulb (fear, lust, anger, greed, lack of self-esteem, and so forth) dims your light.

- ♥ The stories featured in this book will help remove the dust on your light bulb and help you realize you are already absolute perfection, a 1000 – watt bulb!

- ♥ Keep an open mind while reading these true stories. Many may seem unbelievable. Let your heart do the reading, it knows the truth.

- ♥ Start using the Magical Question for all your decisions. You'll quickly discover that you too can do the same and even more!

- ♥ Be in awe of all of creation. Begin today. Make eye contact with everyone. When you do, think, "Each person is a 'Master in disguise,' here to be blessed by me and to bless me in return."

- ♥ Imagine you are holding each person's sacred heart in your blessed hands. The most hardened heart will soften in your presence and fall in LOVE with you.

- ♥ YOU are a Master in disguise. Think like one, talk, walk, dress, feel, act like one and if necessary, fake it until you make it! In no time, every cell of your being will remember the truth, WE ARE ALL DIVINE!

- ♥ There are questions at the end of each chapter for you to ponder on, think about.

- ♥ It is suggested that you have a very special journal to record your answers in. Wouldn't it be nice to have one that had the cover of WWLD? on it?

- ♥ Spiral bound, lined, 7 X 8. journal is available at … www.CafePress.com/CarolinesCreations1
- ♥ They make excellent gifts, for all ages

LOVE
loves to love love.

~ James Joyce ~
https://www.biography.com/people/james-joyce-9358676

LOVE IS IT!

~ It Is So Simple ~

"Simplify what you teach and how you teach it so that everyone else can do the same."

I was hearing that sentence over and repeatedly throughout my meditation - so often that I began questioning if, what, and how I had been teaching had been all wrong.

I spent the rest of the day trying to understand the intent of what I had heard and how I was supposed to apply it. *What am I teaching? Basic universal truths, I hope, and the tools necessary to apply them.*

What and how I share depends upon the need and spiritual level of the person I am sharing with. I've been told I have a gift for taking the most complicated teaching and simplifying it so that everyone, of all ages, can understand and apply it.

I've also heard, "No one else can do what you do. How do you remember everything? How do you know what you know?"

So, if I am doing all that, why am I being asked to simplify what and how I teach and how can others do the same when they say I do the impossible? I know it's not impossible, but they won't believe me when I tell them they can do the same and more! I pondered.

"Look at your tools," I was instructed.

Hmm, yes, I sometimes use tools, writing materials, books, pictures, and so forth. They sound simple enough to me.

"But does everyone else have those same tools?"

Hmm? I had to admit, my average client didn't have Kirlian photographs or energy rods.

As I was grilling myself from every angle possible, I kept receiving thoughts and promptings that would redirect my thinking.

"Review what tool you used to simplify your life," came the next prompt.

I suddenly remembered my painful search beginning when I was about six years of age. I had had many mystical, psychic, spiritual experiences but didn't know what most of them were. Some of them frightened me, and some left me in awe - wanting to know more, wanting to have a personal experience with God. I questioned everyone about everything. Why was I constantly asking why? I drove my teachers crazy with, why this and not that?

I was raised Catholic, but left the church as a teen because no one could prove God existed. "You have to have faith," they would say.

Well, excuse me, if God is so real and everywhere He must be able to be seen and touched and heard and smelled.

I can see, smell, feel, and taste peanut butter so why am I not able to see this all-powerful, all-present, all-knowing force?

Also, everything I am witnessing is more like hell, so 'good-bye' God!"

I stopped looking for God but continued believing that Jesus was a wonderful role model.

I was never taught to ask, "What would Jesus do?" however, it always seemed the most natural thing to do when I had a decision to make, or had to simplify my life for some reason.

The first thing that would pop into my head was my answer and I would act upon it. I often received answers I didn't want to hear, answers that frightened me, and answers that made me laugh hysterically (like the time while I was on a massage course during a forty-five-day fast ... but that is a story in another chapter).

Simplifying everything for me was asking, "What would Jesus have done?" and, as I said, I would do the first thing that came to me.

"Is that way of thinking universally accepted by all religions, all cultures?" (prompt, prompt).

Hmm. No. Not all accept Jesus as I do. By now, I knew that God did exist, in everything and in everyone. *What about using that?* I wondered.

God is not universally acceptable to everyone. Some are unbelievers as I had been; others feel so unworthy that they don't believe God would ever speak to them; finally, others are too afraid to ask a question of a God they have only known as angry, vengeful.

What concept is universally acceptable to all that is also simple to use and to teach? I kept asking myself.

Then it hit me! It was so simple! *GOD IS LOVE! What would LOVE do? Yes! That was it!*

My childlike brain was giddy with delight! That's all I need to share, to teach! And it is something everyone can do! Yes! It requires no tools. The Master never walked around with a bag full of goodies, crystals, runes, cards, and beads. He simply was LOVE. LOVE is all, knows all.

LOVE can talk to, touch, and move anyone-regardless of age, health, religion, and social, economic, educational, or cultural background! Every act is a cry for LOVE. It is the only thing everyone REALLY wants.

It is also all that we are truly made of. It is the 'Krazy Glue' of the universe. It is inside every cell of our being. It knows us … Is us … LOVE us! Oh, I was getting so excited!

"You can do the same as I and even more." The Master's words took on a whole new meaning!

All we had to breathe and be willing to let LOVE take over and it would give us everything we needed simply by asking!

"What if someone was to say they have never known LOVE, have never been touched by LOVE?"

I was ready to answer this one! Not know LOVE! I am not talking about the human emotion.

I am talking about the life force - that which is inside everything and everyone, that which tells the skin how to be skin, the bones how to be bones, the air how to be air, and on and on.

That which is divine ... that is connected to the Creator ... that IS the Creator.

To say you have never been touched by LOVE is to deny every moonbeam, every raindrop, the sunshine, the warm fuzzies caused by a puppy's LOVE or a newborn child, some artwork or music.

"By Jove, I think she's got it!" I could sense my guides and angels doing a tap dance of joy. From that moment on what would LOVE do became my motto, my reply, my credo.

My students often grew tired of hearing that response to their questions; however, it forced them to go inside - to that place of all knowing inside them. It was universal.

Every act on this planet is a cry for LOVE. LOVE is the greatest power ... the ONLY power! LOVE cannot be divided, conquered, or lost.

People do things for two reasons only - LOVE or fear - and when broken down to its pure raw essence, the fear is always a fear of not being loved.

Asking that one question changed everything for me and everyone around me. LOVE, like Jesus, often asked me to do things I did not want to do, was too afraid to do, and didn't have the money, time, energy, or brains to do.

I would simply reply, "If you want me to do this, send me what I need, and I will do it.

I will take the first step, but you had better take over. If I don't get what I need, I will not do it!" I often spoke those words in fear or anger; however, LOVE never failed me.

I also added, "If You don't want me to do this, take this desire, this idea, this feeling (whatever I was experiencing) away," and voilà, it would be gone.

We often pick up on other people's energies and take them on as our own. If I had been doing so, it was suddenly gone!

Human love often failed me; however, divine LOVE never has! How simple and universal my teaching has become!

LOVE ASKS ...

1. Can you tell the difference between LOVE and love?

2. How, when have you been touched by LOVE?

3. Do YOU believe you can do the same as the Master and even more?

LOVE'S BAPTISM OF FIRE
~ Hostage Incident ~

"Do you want to be the first female Physical Education Instructor at Royal Military College?"

The question my career manager asked totally surprised me! I never, in my wildest dreams, thought I would be asked to go to Royal Military College (RMC), Canada's best. Only the 'cream of the crop' in Physical Education and Recreation went to RMC to instruct and train officer cadets.

For the first time in history, the Canadian Armed Forces was about to admit females for officer cadet training, and a female instructor was required. Taking the position at RMC meant my husband would have to follow me for a change.

He had recently retired after serving thirty-one years in the Canadian navy, and had been invited to work for the fire marshal's office as a civilian.

"I'll have to talk it over with my husband," I replied. The move to Kingston, Ontario from Ottawa meant that John Francis (Frank) would have to resume job-hunting, which he didn't savor at his age. I don't know why I was concerned about his reaction; he was as supportive of my career as he had always been.

"I'm sure I can find a job in Kingston" he replied. "This is history in the making! You have to say yes!" So off we went.

I loved our new city and its people. There was always so much to do. The one thing that surprised me was that there were nine prisons in Kingston and area, housing all levels of men and women who had been convicted and sent to jail.

Frank could have simply retired, for good, however, he needed to work and serve as he had done all his adult life. His resume included his experiences as a firefighter, (fire chief, chief instructor at the Canadian Forces Fire School, finally retiring as the Fire Investigation and Arson Specialist at National Defense Headquarters). He was more qualified than most civilian fire chiefs who feared he was after their job, so his applications were always rejected.

He was becoming depressed, thinking he would never work again, when the Department of Correctional Services accepted his resume and began training him as a prison guard, changing his life forever. He went from rescuing and saving innocent human and animal life to dealing with society's rejects, some considered worse than animals. His personality changed. The once very positive, cheerful, productive man became negative, suspicious, and tired. He was spat and urinated on, cursed and threatened.

He came home with stories that would make the hair on the back of your neck stand up - stories 'Joe Public' never would hear, like that fateful day when he had his 'baptism of fire.'

I was at work at the college when, suddenly, I was overcome with a sick panicky feeling in my gut.

I never was one to lose my cool, but I was ready to lose it at that moment. Fear and the sweats totally engulfed me!

I went to my office to breathe and calm myself, all the while asking, *What would LOVE do?* I immediately thought of Frank, and the panic surfaced again.

"Just pray," LOVE said. Pray I did fervently.

Ten minutes later, I sighed a sigh of relief; it was like the weight of the world had been lifted off my shoulders. Peace filled me as quickly as the panic had and Frank was no longer in my thoughts.

Whew! That was intense! I wonder what that was all about. My day continued normally with no one knowing what I had experienced.

Immediately after work we had an unplanned staff meeting. I called Frank to tell him I would be a little late, entirely forgetting the morning's panic attack.

As soon as he answered the phone I asked, "How was your morning?" Normally I would have asked, "How was your day?"

 "How did you know?" he asked.

"Were you in trouble?" I asked, as I remembered the sweats.

"I had my baptism of fire," he replied. I could tell he was still a bit shaken up. "We were transporting four prisoners with three guards. Someone did not do his job properly, because a knife hidden inside the sole of a shoe was used in an attack."

He went on to tell me how his past emergency mentality and ability to react quickly saved his life, and he suffered only a minor cut.

The prisoners were quickly subdued and the only real damage was to his watch, which he kept for a long while as a reminder of the event.

"The whole thing was over in ten minutes, but felt it like an eternity," he sighed.

LOVE inside every cell of our being connects us to all of life on this planet, and it tells us when it needs our help-if we would just listen, if we only knew how.

That was the first of several incidents in which he was involved. I began to recognize these panic attacks, these 'kicks in the gut,' so to speak, for what they really were.

Whenever I felt them, I would immediately begin to pay attention to the first thought that entered my being. That was what I was supposed to do.

Energy was sent to me from someone, and I would respond in the way LOVE guided me to. I must admit, I was very grateful when I finally outgrew that 'knowing' technique, and began to experience my knowing in a gentler way.

LOVE ASKS …

1. Have you ever had a sudden panic attack for no reason?

2. Have you intuitively known when a loved one was in danger?

3. Do you know if the panic you are feeling is yours or someone else

Life is a succession of lessons
which must be lived
to be understood.

~ Helen Keller ~
https://www.biography.com/people/helen-keller-9361967

LOVE'S LITTLE THINGS
~ I Am Told What To Do ~

While I was in the Canadian Armed Forces, I knew what was expected of me, and if I didn't, someone would very quickly advise me. When I left in 1981, I knew I was too young to fully retire, so I wondered what I would do with the rest of my life. I knew I wanted to work with healing so I considered becoming a nurse, a doctor or an athletic trainer; while being pulled toward traditional methods of healing.

Two months of praying and meditating four to five hours a day was frowned upon; however, I was stubborn. I wanted some direction! Nothing was coming to me!

Suddenly my light came on! *What would LOVE do?*

"Watch your dreams," came the reply.

I couldn't wait to get to bed that night! I knew my life was about to change forever. I had my usual night, several dreams, some of them lucid (knowing I am dreaming). I woke up a few times, looked at the clock and wondered when 'the' dream would appear. Nothing was happening, until it was time to get up.

You know that feeling when you are in the middle of a good dream, so good that you don't want it to end; one that you know you must interpret before you move, or you will lose it. *Just give me a few more minutes! This is it! I need to figure it out!* I begged of the dream gods.

He was tall, dark, and handsome; he was dancing, and serenading me. The song was familiar. *I recognize that melody!* I was trying to hear the words he was singing. I was driving myself crazy trying to hear them.

Argh!! It was driving me nuts! I couldn't stay in bed any longer. I had an appointment, and I couldn't be late.

As I showered, I continued analyzing my dream. My question before going to bed was, *What am I supposed to do with my life?*

Viola! I knew the answer!

I had been wasting time trying to hear the lyrics. My answer was in the title of the song, "Little Things Mean A Lot."

I now knew that studying to work in traditional healing would take a lot of time, money, and effort and it would be very limiting. LOVE wanted to work in alternative ways. LOVE liked variety.

That morning I noticed an ad for a reflexology course. The shivers that ran up my spine told me that it was the course I was supposed to take.

Such was the beginning of many little courses that changed my life preparing me to do my life's work. Little things mean a lot - a smile, a thought, or a course.

How many stories have we heard about someone spending just a few more seconds longer than planned with someone, just to realize that doing so helped him or her avoid an accident or other painful incident? I was about to begin doing those little things LOVE would ask me to do.

LOVE ASKS ...

1. What song has been repeated over and over in your mind? Have you been trying to remember the lyrics? Just notice the words you DO remember. THAT IS YOUR MESSAGE.

2. Have you found yourself getting bored with your job? Maybe there is something else waiting for you.

3. What do you think your life's purpose is?

LOVE
is but the discovery of ourselves in others,
and the delight in the recognition.

~ Alexander Smith ~
https://en.wikipedia.org/wiki/Alexander_Smith

LOVE LABELS ME
~ My Tag Line ~

In 1981 I began doing reflexology, and had wonderful results. It was about one year later that I noticed a change in my attitude. I began hoping my clients would forget their appointments. I would start getting tired when they arrived, and tried not to show it. I was getting concerned. *Am I getting lazy? Am I not motivated anymore?*

Even though I was getting fantastic results, I didn't want to do it any more. A course in shiatsu was being offered, and that excited me for a short while. It too began to tire or bore me, just as reflexology had. Then came Mariel healing.

It didn't take me long to see a pattern. As soon as boredom set in, I knew something quicker, easier, more profound and energy efficient was on its way to me. Therapeutic Touch, dream analysis, palliative and pastoral care, the Integrated Awareness Technique, rescue work, the Results System, the Natural Process, and so many more techniques, systems, and practices were learned and applied.

It was wonderful to be qualified in so many techniques, but it became more and more difficult to market myself.

"What do you do?" a potential client would ask.

I didn't know what to say. Many were overwhelmed and feared me when I told them my qualifications.

I asked my students, clients and friends to describe me. Teacher, guru, healer, psychic, clown, minister, dolphin lady and more were their replies.

One student gave we a wonderful gag gift-business cards that said, "Caroline, JUST Caroline, JC for short" I knew I couldn't use that because there was only one JC, didn't you know.

The day a friend called to ask for my help to find an acronym for her new business was the day I learned how LOVE would describe or label me.

LOVE gave me an acronym … it said I was a S.H.E.P.H.E.R.D. … A

Spiritual
Human
Empowering
People's
Hearts
Everywhere to
Remember their
Divinity

WOW! I was humbled! I was in awe of this interpretation of shepherd however, quickly discovered it was not going to work with everyone.

Some would ask, "Do you have sheep?"

"Sometimes we do," I would reply, telling them of my John's LOVE of animals.

I Loved LOVE's label, but I noticed some people were very uncomfortable with it; who was I to call myself that, in the spiritual, consulting sense. Some thought it was sacrilegious. After all, there is only one Shepherd, don't you now, Jesus.

Why would LOVE give me that label if I couldn't use it? I wondered.

"You needed to get an understanding of what a shepherd is, who can be one, and to awaken others to that role-the role they play in the lives of others," LOVE responded.

I began to realize EVERYONE IS A SHEPHERD. A shepherd is a protector, a leader, a guide.

Church persons, teachers, parents, politicians, businesses, yes, even gang leaders could be considered shepherds with a flock of followers. I'm sure there are some who follow you, want to be with you, listen to you

Can you imagine what the world would be like if each of us acted as a... S.H.E.P.H.E.R.D.! What a different world we would live in.

Great! I still have a problem saying what I do. Again, I called upon LOVE to guide me.

I heard, "Just ask your next client."

Two hours after LOVE gave me that thought, my next session with a client ended with both of us 'flying higher than a kite.' It had been the type of session where I felt I should be the one paying for services rendered.

LOVE's energy was so high, so powerful, so beautiful and humbling! I was moved as much as my client was. I was moved to ask her how she would describe me.

"I know what you are," she said excitedly. "You're my Spiritual Electrician. You reached into my heart and turned my light on!"

Wow! It was perfect! It was simple, cute, non-threatening. It became my elevator speech - a 10 second or less blurb of what one does that makes people want to ask for your business card.

Now, when people ask what I am or what I do, I say, "I'm a Spiritual Electrician, I reach into people's hearts and turn their light on!" Their eyes just light up.

"What if my light is already on?" some ask.

"I can help you increase your wattage, change the color of your light, help you with re-wiring or give you tools to clean the dust off your light bulb. I can also help you understand why your light chooses to light up a closet, instead of a classroom".

For a while I had no problem with it. It was easy to remember, no threatening, fun ... until ... I became President of the Sudbury Business and Professional Women's Club! It was too woo woo for these conservative business women. Again, I had to ask LOVE for help.

The time-consuming search and introspection that took place was so necessary and valuable.

I kept being asked by mentors what my niche, tribe was. What type of person did I want to serve? I kept asking them, "What was Jesus' niche? None of them could answer that. I often heard some think, "Are you comparing yourself to Jesus?"

After much soul searching I KNEW it had to connect with my soul's sole purpose, to make people aware of their divinity and all my actions had to center in LOVE.

FINALLY, I had it ... I AM LOVE'S DIVINE MESSENGER!

My niche was YOU! You are in my flock!

Everyone, all ages, all cultures, beliefs, mentalities, religions! LOVE wanted to give everyone a message!

I now look at people in a different light, and wonder who is in their flock, and wonder if they are aware that each of them is a S.H.E.P.H.E.R.D.

LOVE ASKS ...

1. I ask you, who is in your flock?

2. How can you be a better shepherd?

3. How does LOVE want you to turn someone's light on?

*Joy goes against
the foundations of mathematics:
it multiplies when we divide.*

~ Paulo Coelho ~
https://www.biography.com/people/paulo-coelho-5524

LOVE'S WAKE UP CALL!
~ I Am Not Lazy ~

I had been retired from the military for months, and was still hearing those words every morning, "Wakey Wakey, time to get up!"

I am retired! I don't want to get up! I am s-o-o-o-o-o tired! Am I getting lazy, or does my body need the rest after so many years of driving it into the ground as a physical education instructor?

My husband had retired from two careers and was still getting up every morning to go to work at his third.

He is eighteen years older than I. He is the one who should be staying in bed. I am the one who should be going to work. But ... I am so tired. I kept arguing. What would LOVE do? I wondered.

"Play red light, green light," came the answer.

What? Red light. Green light! I hadn't played that since I was seven years old. Red light always meant STOP! Stay in bed; your body needs one extra hour of sleep ...guilt free. Green light always meant GO! Get your tush out of bed, you have work to do.

OK then, let's play red light green light. Which light would LOVE give me? No! A green light! I don't want a green light. I am tired ... I just want to sleep for ten years. Ok, let's try two out of three ... what would LOVE see? Aieeee! Another green light! Ok ... three out of five ... what would LOVE do? NOT AGAIN!

Ok! Ok! I get the message. You had better zap me, do something to me! I grumbled to my guides and angels. *I will take the first step. I will begin by getting out of bed, but if I don't feel energized in the next three steps, back to bed I go-to stay!*

I made the first move, and by the time I took the second step I felt energized and ready to roll. In fifteen minutes I had done my toilet, dressed, and had a bite to eat; when the phone rang.

"Caroline, we need you at so and so's."

It never failed me. Every time I got the green light, I would get zapped, fired up, and was always ready when called to serve, which always happened within the half hour.

There were times I did get the red light ... two to date! The first time, I slept the sleep of babes and woke up exactly one hour later feeling refreshed.

When my husband came home that day and asked what I had done with my day I sheepishly said, "I slept in an extra hour."

He and LOVE must have been on the same team because he responded with, "Good. Your body must have needed the extra rest."

Wow! It worked!

Why don't you play red light green light the next time you don't feel like getting out of bed or making other decisions?

You must always be willing to take the first step; LOVE will take over and do the rest. Red light, green light was one of the first ways LOVE gave me my wake-up call.

LOVE ASKS ...

1. Have you found a way to boost your battery when you felt too tired to get out of bed?

2. What do you do to get the desire to do something you don't want to do?

3. Do you let someone guilt you into doing something you don't want to do?

*The sign of a beautiful person is
that they always see beauty in others.*

~ Omar Suleiman ~
https://www.infoplease.com/people/omar-suleiman

LOVE LOVES LETTUCE
~ Something Yucky Becomes Yummy ~

I was hungry and wanted my soda pop and chocolate bar. I thought, *I'll give that LOVE thing a try and see if it works.*

When I asked, "What would LOVE eat?" I was not impressed! The idea of having a salad popped into my head.

I am NOT a salad person! I don't want your stupid salad, I want my pop and chocolate bar I mentally argued. But more than doing what I want, I wanted to do what LOVE wanted, so I challenged LOVE, *If you want me to have this salad you had better zap it, do something to it to make it tasty because if I eat this salad and it doesn't satisfy my appetite I am going to eat my chocolate bar! Are you listening God?"* I was SO ticked off.

Talking to guides, angels and LOVE was a new experience for me and I was really grateful that they were more gracious and patient than I.

Well! LOVE must have done something to it because it took me almost an hour to eat that salad. NOT because it was bad ... but because ... it was the tastiest, most delicious salad I had ever eaten! I almost sucked it to death! I thought I had died and gone to heaven and I am not exaggerating. It was almost orgasmic ... hee hee.

The next time I wanted my pop and chocolate bar and asked, *What would LOVE eat?* I thought LOVE would give me another salad, nope!

I saw myself eating a bite of chocolate, then a second, and then no more. Ah! I had been satisfied, and without guilt!

LOVE knows everything. It knew within half an hour a friend would phone and ask, "Can I come over for coffee?"

LOVE knew if I had not had my caffeine fix I would have been in the middle of my caffeine withdrawal headaches, which I used to have a lot of, and I probably would have replied, "I'm not feeling too good. Can I have a rain check?"

LOVE knew my friend wasn't strong enough to say, "I need help." She was suicidal, so LOVE gave me the fix I needed so I would be available to help her over the next four hours.

Asking the LOVE question was working better than I thought it would. It hadn't failed me yet!

LOVE ASKS ...

1. What is your favorite food / addiction?

2. Would you be willing to give it up?

3. Would you trust LOVE IF it asked you to eat something else?

LOVE USES MY WEAKNESS TO SHOW ITS STRENGTH
~ Forty-Five-Day Fast Is A Breeze ~

When I was a teen, the forty-five-day period in the Catholic Church just before Easter called Lent (when one made sacrifices), had always been one of my favorite times. My high school was just beyond the church so going to mass before school was an easy sacrifice to make especially because I enjoyed smelling the incense, singing the songs, praying in Latin and contemplating the meaning of the pictures on the stained-glass windows.

When I was younger, hearing we were the ones and only ones favored in God's eyes upset me a great deal. I couldn't understand a God that would LOVE only some of His children. The Church asking for money confused me when it was already so wealthy and should have been giving to the poor instead of taking from them.

During Lent I would say my rosary every night and often fell asleep on the floor before I finished, only to wake up feeling the guilt of being imperfect and disappointing God … again! I was so afraid of God when I was young that if I stole a nickel I would really punish myself before He could.

I remember one Lenten period when I stole a dime from a friend. I wanted to go to confession, but I knew the priest could see who was on the other side of the screen in the confessional, maybe not clearly, but enough to make me afraid of being recognized.

I figured a way to get around that, to avoid being shamed.

I entered the confessional wearing a hat with big sequins and I knew he would remember me as the very bad girl who had stolen a dime. I felt he could easily figure out who I was outside the confessional because of the shiny sequins on my hat.

I made my confession, got my penance and waited for the priest to slide the little door over the screen. I quickly took off my sparkly hat and put on a plain scarf. *He won't be able to recognize me now!* I thought.

I left the confessional, said my penance with relief, grateful for the idea of disguising myself.

Sometime after that, I realized, if the priest had really wanted to find who that bad girl was, he just had to look around. I was the only child with four adults in the church at the time and because I was so afraid of getting caught, so afraid of being recognized, I wasn't thinking straight.

I tried everything to get to know God on a personal level. I knew what peanut butter tasted, looked, smelled, and felt like and I wanted to know God in the same way.

No such luck. All I kept seeing was anger, fear, abuse, poverty, judgment, and loneliness all around me.

I became so disillusioned I decided God did not exist.

I stopped going to church, stopped praying, and started skipping school. I finally ran away from home at sixteen. I became a live-in housekeeper / nanny for an Italian couple with three children. I stayed with them for one year.

I then joined the military because I believed I was too dumb to get a job and nobody would want to marry an ugly redhead with freckles. Joining the military allowed me to get away, be on my own and still have someone take care of me, indirectly. I spent the next twelve years in the military learning how to teach, lead, and survive. I had no time for God until LOVE knew it was time for me to wake up to my true passion.

Two years at National Defense Medical Centre (NDMC) in the Physiotherapy department helping mend sick and broken bodies helped me realize I was tired of showing others how to kill, I wanted to teach them how to heal.

I then learned to meditate and my search for God was rekindled with a desperate passion.

It would take two more years before I was ready to leave the military. I continued to mediate for hours daily.

I lived to serve LOVE and before Easter of 1982 I realized I hadn't done anything for lent since I was a teen. *What would LOVE do for Lent?* I wondered in meditation.

I heard the words loud and clear, "Fast … He will use your weakness to show His strength."

Well, there was no doubt now! I really loved food at that time, so fasting would be a challenge. I remembered Jesus fasted for forty-five days and He said, "You can do the same as I and even more," and I knew He wasn't a liar; I believed I could do it.

My priest said, "Caroline, you don't have to give up food completely. That's not what the Church wants. Just eat two meals a day instead of three. Just cut back." My doctor said, "Woman, you are crazy. If you fast and pass out on the street, I will just step right over you." I knew he would never do that; he was just trying to impress upon me the danger of going without solid food for so long. My husband was smart enough to say nothing. He knew this stubborn redhead would do it, just to spite him. So, I fasted for Lent.

For the first eight days I drank nothing but water. Whenever I was hungry I would have a little talk with LOVE. *If You want me to stay on this fast, this glass of water will satisfy my appetite; however, if I am still hungry after drinking this glass of water that means I am supposed to stop the fast and eat solid food.* I would take a few sips of water and be full!

On or about the eleventh day, I allowed myself to drink juice. During this time, I was still running a few kilometers a day, taking a massage course, attending banquets, meeting friends in restaurants, and still managed to stay on the fast. I had many wonderful, mystical, spiritual experiences, but I also went to hell and back.

It is not something I would recommend for the unprepared. I relived painful memories that needing healing. Childhood experiences, involving strange breathing techniques, began again.

I became lost in space and time; I often appeared mentally unstable because of the extreme mood swings.

I became aware of lost souls, and of being a rescue–worker. I was visited by the spirit of future teachers and others, and was the instrument in helping others heal, and on and on.

As frightening and disturbing as most of it was, I knew it was all on-the- job training for the work I was destined to do.

I knew instinctively that everything I experienced was preparing me for the next person or challenge I was to meet. No one, nothing, came into my life for no reason.

The universe did not waste energy that way. All I read, saw, felt, heard, tasted, and experienced in any way was necessary.

I learned about Theresa Neumann's death in Germany when I was about 12 years-old, and that planted a seed in me. She was known for eating nothing more than the Eucharistic wafer each day. She also suffered the stigmata (the sufferings of Christ) I had a deep knowing that someday I would be like her. I would not have to eat.

During one meditation, I remember wondering, *what would it feel like to wear a crown of thorns?* I immediately began feeling sharp pains in my head.

Panic! *No! No! I change my mind. It hurts too much.* Thank God LOVE did not force that upon me. I had to be more careful with my curiosity. Reading Autobiography of a Yogi by Paramahansa Yogananda felt like going home. In it, a young girl was considered a glutton, and often ridiculed by her husband's family until she sat under a Bodhi tree and vowed she would not move until God showed her how to take her nutrition, prana directly out of the air. She was shown certain breathing techniques, which sustained her throughout her adult life. She began at about twelve years of age and continued until her death sixty years later. Again, I had a deep knowing that I would not need food to live.

When I remembered we are spiritual beings having a human experience and the body is the spacesuit that makes us visible, I knew I, Spirit, could do without food. A book, Ton Corps Te Parle, Ecoute Le (Your Body Is Speaking To You, Listen to It) said, "Many people on the spiritual path believe they must become vegetarian but their bodies are not always ready, so they fail, or it is always a struggle."

All foods have different vibrations feeding us at different levels.

1. If you can eat a meal with pork and be satisfied, you are ready for higher vibration food …beef, red meats

2. If you can eat a meal with red meats and be satisfied, you are now ready for fish and poultry … white meats.
3. If you can eat a meal with fish or poultry and be satisfied, you are now ready for fruit and vegetables.
4. If you can eat a salad and be satisfied, you are now ready for a handful of seeds, nuts or grain.
5. If a handful of seeds, nuts or grains satisfies you, you are now ready to become
6. A breatharian, one who takes his/her food, life-force, energy, prana, directly from the source … air, spirit.

All I experienced would be on-the-job training for the work I was destined to do, and that forty-five-day fast was the easiest I ever did. I have done many shorter fasts since then but none came from the deep knowing LOVE gave me … that I could do this and even more!

SPECIAL NOTE: When moved by spirit, by LOVE, to not eat, the body does not experience illness and pain. It often becomes healthier or remains the same. Many who have done so, have amazingly ample bodies. They are not under weight; and they lead full, active lives. Strangers seeing them for the first time would not believe they don't eat food because they look so fit, so normal.

On the other hand, there are many who do not eat because of emotional, human issues.

These are the people who become ill, anorexic, bulimic and so forth. There is a big difference. When motivated by true LOVE, everything and anything is possible.

LOVE ASKS ...

1. How long do you think you could SAFELY go without eating?

2. What level do you think you are at when it comes to eating? (According to the levels 1 to 6)

3. Would you be willing to fast just one day each week?

LOVE IS HYSTERICAL
~ So Is Jesus ~

During my forty-five-day fast I took an eight-week massage course with eleven other women. The majority were painfully shy - especially me. Class after class we became braver, and by the fourth class we boldly moved around in our panties and tightly wrapped sheets, looking like mummies. We didn't make a move without our security blankets. The ladies kept telling me I had a body to die for: shapely, solid, petite-the envy of every woman. My physical education background had kept me fit, and my 45 days fast had trimmed off the last traces of any fat I had. Did I feel proud? Feel ok? No way. I had such an inferiority complex I never saw myself as desirable, or even average. I always felt like the 'ugly duckling.'

At the end of the seventh class, the instructor suggested we have a body awareness session, followed by a potluck for our last class. The tension in the room could have been cut with a knife!

What was a body awareness session? Our fears were quickly confirmed! A body awareness session consisted of every person being nude and taking a turn standing in the middle of the circle. Those sitting in the outer ring would tell the one in the center what they liked about her body. One could enter the center not liking her big hips, and exit feeling they were wonderfully soft and sensuous.

The intention was to see our bodies in a different, more positive light.

"The previous class of males and females had a body awareness session and totally enjoyed it," our instructor continued. "They then sat down on the floor, still in the nude and fed each other food brought in for the potluck. Why don't we do the same to celebrate your growth and beauty?" she asked.

Gasp! You could have heard a pin drop on her carpeted floor. Everyone stopped breathing and panicked!

She wisely added, "Just think about it, and if only one refuses, we will not do it."

Ask me if I was tossing and turning over this one! I was just beginning to realize that maybe I did have an 'OK' body. It was nothing to be ashamed of, so why did I feel so uncomfortable?

I could understand feeding each other. We would learn what being handicapped and dependent upon someone else to feed you was like. Especially if it was someone you did not like, feeding you food you did not want. I kept turning it over and over in my head and my nonexistent stomach (as the massage teacher called it), was beginning to feel the return of ulcers. It was class night, and I still hadn't found peace. Suddenly, my light came on!

What would LOVE do? I suddenly broke out into hysterical laughter!

The thought of Jesus sitting there with his family jewels hanging out and his mother feeding him was so preposterous I couldn't stop laughing. It wasn't because He was ashamed of his body, but because it wasn't appropriate ... not for this class.

My answer would very easily be a guilt free, "No!"

I was the first one asked, and when I told my story in detail, you could hear the giggles and a sigh of relief. The body awareness session would have to be done in the privacy of our own homes and not here. We did our massages, got dressed, enjoyed our potluck, trying to feed each other occasionally and remained 'fast' friends. (Please excuse the pun.)

A big smile crosses my face every time I think of that experience. It was so nice to know LOVE and Jesus were on the same wavelength, and that they had a great sense of humor.

LOVE ASKS ...

1. Have you ever been faced with a dilemma and found yourself laughing out loud at the solution because it was so simple or obvious?

2. How do YOU feel about your body? Could you have done a body awareness session with others?

3. Could you stand nude, in front of a mirror in the privacy of your own home? If not, why not?

When you give and carry out acts of kindness, it's as though something inside your body responds and says, 'Yes, this is how I ought to feel.'

~ Rabbi Harold Kushner ~
http://content.time.com/time/arts/article/0,8599,1545682,00.html

LOVE GOES TO THE MOVIES
~ Husband Learns Important Lesson ~

I had been away for three weeks and was looking forward to enjoying the comforts of my own apartment with my husband. It sure was nice to travel, yet so-o-o-o nice to get home.

One way I relax and unwind is to go to the theatre. The energy of a large audience has always been part of the enjoyment. Three days after being home, I was thinking of taking in a new movie I really wanted to see. I asked my husband if he wanted to go. I was not ready for his reaction.

"You know I don't like movies! You've been away for three weeks, why don't you just stay home with me and watch a movie on TV?"

A heated discussion began about his not liking movies and feeling forced to go just to please me. I had not been aware of the way he felt until that moment. In the past, when I had been away, I always gave in to his request that I stay home, but this time I really wanted to go. So, I asked, *What would LOVE do?* and saw myself going to the theater.

He was not happy! He huffed and puffed and probably would have blown the house down if he could have. I began to doubt LOVE's decision, but asked for the courage to go. Suddenly I was out the door and on my way.

I had a great time with friends I hadn't seen in a long while and had totally forgotten about my husband's mood until I returned home. LOVE surprised me again!

I tiptoed into the living room and was greeted by, "You know I was really angry with you for choosing a movie over me and thought, to hell with you. I began to read a book I had wanted to read and then began to realize I can entertain myself and have a good time without you; that I didn't need to depend on you to make me happy. I think it was a good thing you went to the movie tonight."

You could have knocked me over with a feather!

One other time a similar scene played itself out; again, he was upset.

I never made it to the theater … I ended up counseling someone on the way there and my husband had an unexpected visitor, so we both had a fulfilling evening.

At other times, I had to go to the theater to have a healing triggered by the movie, or just to relax or to meet someone who eventually hired me to do a presentation. After many years of pushing each other's 'movie' buttons, we both learned a lot. My main lesson was, if I didn't honor my desires and needs, why should anyone else?

Once again LOVE knew it all and knew I loved my movies and popcorn and used that to help me grow!

LOVE ASKS ...

1. Have you ever done anything someone else did not want you to do?

2. What were the repercussions?

3. Would you do so again?

*The two most important days
in your life are
the day you are born
and
the day you find out why.*

~ Mark Twain ~
https://www.biography.com/people/mark-twain-9512564

LOVE MOVES ME TO TRUST
~ It Takes Two To Fight ~

I can't remember what the argument was about, but this time I was not going to let myself feel responsible for everything. I had just begun to learn what co-dependency was and saw myself as a classic example of one who needed to fix things for others before I could feel good about myself; always feeling responsible for their happiness. Often experienced by the first-born child of a large family, like I was.

I decided right there and then if he wanted to argue he would have to do so by himself! I went to my office to drown myself in work. Two hours flew by. Suddenly, his face popped into my mind and I thought, *Oh, gee, I forgot about him. I wonder if he is still angry. What should I do? What would LOVE do?* I immediately saw myself running into the kitchen, grabbing him by the cheeks and saying, "Oh, you're so cute when you're angry." *Oh yeah, right! I don't think so!*

"Trust," LOVE whispered.

I took a deep breath, went into the kitchen, grabbed his cheeks and said, "Oh, you're so cute when you're angry." He began laughing and asked,

"How did you know?"

"Know what?" I asked, as I exhaled with relief.

"How did you know I was just about to ask for your forgiveness?"

Caroline did not know, but LOVE knew, and made it easy for both of us to kiss and make up.

It could have let me stay where I was and let him come to me, however, I believe I needed to learn to trust LOVE in the little matters of the heart to prepare me for greater challenges in the future.

It made me think of Olga Whorrell, a wonderful healer, who is no longer with us.

I had had the privilege of dining with her, and asked how she handled the emotions of the horror stories she was often presented with.

She said she had simply learned to trust LOVE in the little things.

"I simply let go and let God handle it," she repeated more than once. "I have nothing to do with it. I just step aside and let LOVE do the work."

Now that is trust! I was praying for this kind of trust. I suppose I had just passed a little test with my husband. I had also learned how to be less co-dependent. I was NOT responsible for his happiness, he was!

LOVE ASKS ...

1. Are YOU co-dependent? Do you feel responsible for people's happiness, always needing to fix things for others?

2. Have you noticed that when you fixed things for someone, those people never learn to take care of themselves and often begin to resent you?

3. How do you feel when someone tries to take over, help you and won't let you try things on your own/?

Learn to appreciate what you have,
before time makes you appreciate
what you had.

~ Unknown ~

LOVE SAYS GO
~ Aunt Finally Goes Home ~

Aunt Marie's life was very difficult. She was Dad's only sister, and being female in those days meant she had to help her mother with the housework, cooking, and generally taking care of the men and the home. Dad's mom died when he was fifteen so Aunt Marie became the woman of the house in her early twenties.

Dad's father, his deaf and mute uncle, and four brothers were now Aunt Marie's responsibility. As if that wasn't enough, one of Dad's brothers had been injured and was confined to a wheelchair most of his life, unable to take care of his basic needs. Aunt Marie cleaned, cooked, sewed, and performed all the duties required of the woman of the house, giving up her own social life until much later, when she finally met and married a wonderful man who had children of his own. Once again Aunt Marie took care of loved ones until her spouse died.

She had always been a heavy woman and developed many medical problems later in life. Diabetes, broken hips, leukemia, and other medical issues resulted in her becoming a permanent resident of the hospital.

Years before that, I remember sharing a room with her for one week at the Princess Margaret Hospital in Toronto, renowned for cancer treatments.

We exchanged stories, jokes and wishes; laughed, cried, and prayed together.

It was then that I found out how much Aunt Marie wanted to die, to go back home to God.

"I have been praying, for thirty years, to die," she said more than once. "I don't know why God is keeping me here in all this pain. I have suffered enough."

She told me about her experience seeing the famous evangelistic healer Kathryn Kuhlman. There were thousands of people there; many who were seated around her were healed, but she was not.

"I guess He's got more work for you to do," I replied, not knowing what more to say.

"When I die, I do not want a wake, a funeral, nothing. Just cremate me," she said. She even had it in her will that there was not to be a viewing, of any kind.

Aunt Marie had been a resident in the hospital for several years when I got the call. "Auntie Marie is gone," Mom said.

"How's Dad doing?" I asked.

"You know how he is, he never even went to see her in the hospital," Mom said sadly.

"When is the funeral going to be?" I continued, not wanting to think of Dad and the pain he must be going through. He and his family all had trouble visiting loved ones in hospitals.

"There isn't going to be a funeral, or even a wake," Mom replied.

I had already made plans to travel home that weekend, for other reasons, and wondered whether I should leave four days earlier. *What would LOVE do?* I wondered.

"Go home," came the answer.

"I'm coming home," I replied. "I will leave first thing in the morning."

I drove eight hours, alone with my memories of my aunt and our talks. I had not managed to get to know her as much as I could have, but I did get to know some things her family never knew.

When I entered the house, Mom and Dad greeted me with hugs and the usual offerings of food.

"When is the wake?" I asked. I wasn't about to let my aunt go without at least having a family gathering to celebrate her life, to say thank you, and farewell.

"What wake?" Mom asked. "Even if she wanted one, aren't you rushing things a little?"

"What do you mean?" I asked. "You called and told me Auntie Marie died yesterday so I came home earlier than planned."

"I never said she died!" Mom replied. "I said Auntie Marie went into a coma again."

I could have sworn I heard Mom say my aunt had died! *Why did my ears hear that?*

Why did I have to come home earlier than planned?

"Dad, have you been to see Auntie Marie yet?" I asked.

"No, you know how I hate hospitals," he snapped.

LOVE moved me to get me here; there had to be a reason. What was it?

"What would LOVE do?" was whispered in my ear.

"Get your coat and hat on, Dad. We're going to the hospital now," I ordered. I was surprised at my tone of voice; I was not going to accept any refusal.

As we traveled in the car, I told Dad, "Hearing is the last thing to go when someone is about to die, Dad. The patient hears everything that is said, even when in a coma. It's time to tell your sister she can go. She doesn't have to take care of you anymore."

"What the hell are you talking about?" Dad grumbled. "She hasn't taken care of us for years".

"She may not have been cooking and sewing for you, but she has continued to feel responsible for all of you. It's time to say, Thank you for all your sacrifice. You can go home now."

"You're crazy," Dad mumbled as we approached the hospital. It was late, and visiting hours were over, however, I knew we would be allowed in. LOVE would not get us there and shut the door in our face. We were allowed in. The nurse directed us to her room.

"Remember what to say, Dad. Give her thanks and permission to go," I whispered.

"She doesn't need my permission," he replied angrily.

"Just humor me. Will it hurt to say thank you and good-bye?"

He took a deep breath and began speaking. He was fantastic!

I felt as though I was intruding in a very intimate moment between a brother and his sister so I quietly left the room.

The visit was short and left us reflecting as we shared a quiet ride home. Aunt Marie had been praying for thirty years to die.

Once Dad gave her permission, she was gone in a matter of hours. I figured LOVE knew what my aunt needed, and it was time. LOVE used me to get the job done.

I consider it a privilege to serve someone about to return home. Good-bye Auntie Marie. Many thanks for all your caring and years of unselfish service.

LOVES ASKS …

1. Have you said all your thank you's and good byes?

2. IF you dislike hospitals, would you visit a loved one?

3. Did you know, hearing is the last thing to go? Patients hear every word spoken, even when in a coma.

LOVE CALLS HOME
~ Win Win Situation For Everyone ~

My mother was about to have much-needed surgery and I wanted to be there for her. She had been quite ill for the several years and I wasn't sure if this would be the last time I would see her.

"It would be so much easier if you could go to Sudbury next week instead of this one," my boss told me. "The General is visiting, and you are the one heading the project he is here to see. If you went next week, I could give you ten days leave instead of seven."

"I know," I replied. "I appreciate the predicament this is putting you in, however this may be the last time I see my mom alive."

He approved my pass, and I began preparations. The next day, I was packed and ready to leave. *Did I have everything?* I checked my bags a second time. I putzed a bit more. *Why am I hesitating?* I wondered. *Is it because I don't want to face the possibility that this might be the last time I see Mom?*

I had to get going sooner or later. It was best to do the eight-hour trip in daylight, so I finally said goodbye to my husband and hustled my tush out the door. I had been driving for about fifteen minutes, was out of the city and onto the highway heading for Sudbury when the thought of my mom became so strong I could not put it off.

Oh my God! Don't tell me she has died! I cried. *Was this feeling just the fear of losing Mom or did it just happen?*

What would LOVE do? I wondered.

"Call Sudbury," came the reply. Five minutes later I pulled off the highway into a service center to use the phone.

"I'm so glad you called," Mom said. "I just called your place about twenty minutes ago and Frank told me you were already on the road."

"What's up?" I asked, relieved she was still alive.

"I just wanted to call you and tell you not to come today but to come next week. The surgeon is not available until next week," she explained. "By the way, what made you call?"

"I got such a strong pull to call you that I couldn't resist it," I replied. It's a good thing I did, because if I had gone all the way home I probably would have stayed and my boss would not have been too happy.

"Go back home," Mom replied. "I'm ok for now. See you next week."

I returned home and to work that afternoon, much to my boss's surprise and relief. I managed to take care of the VIP and was granted the extra time off when I began my second trip to Sudbury.

To an outsider, this whole story might not seem like a big thing, but LOVE knew I would not be needed until the next week when the three extra days were truly appreciated because Mom had more difficulty in recovery than expected and I was needed in Sudbury, not Kingston.

I still am amazed how LOVE knows exactly where each of us should be at all times.

LOVE ASKS ...

1. Have you listened to your 'hunches'?

2. Would you recognize them now?

3. Have you regretted not doing so?

I set out on a journey of love,
seeking truth, peace and understanding.
I am still learning.

~ Muhammad Ali ~
https://www.biography.com/people/muhammad-ali-9181165

LOVE VISITS THE MORGUE
~ LOVE Knows Where LOVE Needs To Be ~

"Will you take my place on duty?" asked Debbie.

Changing schedules was permitted with the Victim Crisis Assistance and Referral Services (VCARS) if the replacement was qualified. I had been on the team longer than Debbie, so it wasn't a problem. The VCARS program was partnered with the city police. Whenever the police were called to an incident, the volunteers of VCARS were called in to assist the victims, enabling the police to go to their next call. VCARS served in all cases, whether it be rape, break and enter, an accident … anything and everything except a domestic violence or drunkenness.

It was two days before Christmas, and Debbie would be able to travel home for the holidays two days earlier if I said yes. I was hoping to do some last-minute shopping and baking, and didn't really want to do her shift.

The two-hour ride home after her shift wouldn't be hard to do! I thought, a little perturbed. *What would LOVE do?* I asked.

"Say yes," came the answer.

But I don't want to! I argued. *Ok! Send me what I need and I will do it!* I told LOVE. Little did I know, it would be necessary to replace Debbie.

Ten minutes after saying yes to Debbie, I received a call from the police. I had to escort a family to the morgue to identify their eight-year-old son who had just been run over by a train!

Oh, my God! What will be left of him? What must the family be going through! The father had been out on a Christmas pass from one of the minimum-security prisons and had decided to take his son ice fishing with him and his brother. The boy was thrilled. He loved to fish and he loved being with his dad and uncle ... with the men.

His mom and eleven-year-old sister stayed home to do some Christmas baking. Dad was going to be home for Christmas - the first time in a long while.

They whistled and talked. The boy couldn't be happier. Dad decided to take a shortcut by walking along the railway track.

What was that sound? The roar was getting closer! A train was coming! There was only one thing they could do to get to safety – jump across the track!

They jumped and fell to the ground. Before he could get up, the father saw his son's boot on the ground ... on the other side.

No! It couldn't be! He had to have made it! His boot just fell off as he jumped! Maybe he fell backwards and didn't get sucked in by the train! the father prayed.

"No-o-o-o-o!" He screamed and screamed and screamed and screamed! It was impossible to hold him. He went crazy.

By the time I was called, the child had been taken to the hospital morgue. I personally had seen many dead bodies but never one that had been run over by a train.

It took some time to gather everyone, to calm them down and to prepare them for the nightmare that was about to take place. His sister insisted on going in with her parents. They allowed it, knowing it would be the last time she would have a chance to say good-bye to her little brother.

The child and family's angels must have been with them because the greater damage had been done below the neck. They managed to wipe some blood off his face but couldn't hide the bruises and cuts. Our hearts felt like they were being ripped out of our bodies. I didn't know this boy, but I could tell he was special.

I remained with that family the entire day. I continued to serve them through the funeral, Christmas, and a few days after that. Not something normally done by VCARS volunteers.

It was apparent why LOVE asked me to take Debbie's place that fateful day. She could have chosen someone else to ask for the favor, but she asked me.

I was trained in palliative and pastoral care, had worked in hospitals, had seen many terrible accidents, and had gone to more funerals than I cared to count.

Debbie had never been to one funeral in her life, nor had she seen a dead body. LOVE knew where it needed to be and knew which one could best serve. I was glad I had said yes to Debbie's request. The shopping didn't get done, but it no longer mattered!

LOVE ASKS ...

1. Have you seen a dead body?

2. Are you ok going to funerals?

3. Would you consider volunteering with VCARS?

LOVE NEEDS ME
~ It Sends A Message ~

She needed to get away from her alcoholic, drug-addicted, much older, abusive husband who had lost one leg to disease and was about to lose the other. Sally wanted to get her life in order before her husband dragged her down any further.

She moved in with us and began taking assertiveness training and self-esteem courses. She was also undergoing a series of tests and examinations by psychologists to determine the best treatment for her depression. I dropped her off at the doctor's office. "I'll call when I'm finished," Sally told me. "I'll probably be here till 8 p.m."

"No problem," I replied and drove home. *Ahhh! A few hours with nothing to do. Refreshing.* I thought. I picked up the newspaper, sat down in my comfy chair and promptly fell asleep.

Suddenly my eyes popped open! *What time is it? Oh my God, it's 8:30! I must go get Sally; but, she said she would call. Why hasn't she called? Is she in trouble?* Two women had been raped in the area near the doctor's office in recent weeks and the buzz around the neighborhood was that the rapist could be a physician.

Well, my mind went everywhere with that thought! Around 8:45 p.m. I was in a panic. *What would LOVE do?* I wondered. *Sally needs me*, was the only thought that came.

I called the doctor's office and let the phone ring fifteen times. *Maybe I had called the wrong number.* I dialed again. This time I let the phone ring thirty times. Still no answer. *She must be in trouble.* I grabbed my keys and ran out the door. I didn't take my purse or any money for a phone call. I was moving fast and nothing was going to stop me. *Sally needs me!* I rolled through stop signs and ran red lights. I couldn't get there fast enough.

I finally arrived. Sally was coming out of the doctor's office looking totally peaceful and unruffled. "I just called the house and when no one answered I figured you'd be out here." Sally said as she got into the car.

"Are you all right?" I asked gasping for air, not realizing I had been holding my breath for quite a while.

"Sure. Why? Are you all right?" she asked. "You look like you've seen a ghost."

I told her what had happened. She repeated she was ok. I drove home in silence, very confused. I had to wait until the next morning to find out why Sally needed me.

My staff meeting was interrupted by a phone call from my husband. "Come home, Sally needs you."

My stomach lurched; I dropped the phone and almost passed out. Frank and Sally had just returned from shopping. Frank was unloading the groceries when the phone rang.

Sally ran to pick it up and heard, "Is this Mrs. Smith?"

"Yes," Sally replied. "I am Detective _____ from the Sault. I am calling to tell you your husband hanged himself last night around 8:45 p.m."

Sally screamed and passed out. Frank ran in wondering what had happened. He picked up the phone and demanded to know who was speaking and what had been said. When he found out he was furious!

"The inconsiderate idiot who would call a person to deliver that kind of message over the phone without relaying it through a minister, a family member, or calling the local police to intervene should be shot!" he fumed. He was furious, but would deal with it later. Right now, Sally needed attention.

That's when he called me to come home, "Sally needs you."

LOVE knew what was happening. It knew Sally would need me and prepared me. I was sad that I had not had more experience with interpreting these kinds of messages.

I probably would have gotten a clearer understanding, but on the other hand if LOVE had wanted me to know more, it would have given me more. LOVE knew all. All I knew was LOVE needed me because Sally needed me!

LOVE ASKS ...

1. Do you know anyone who has committed suicide?

2. Do you think the Detective did the right thing when in the way he delivered Sally's news?

3. Have you panicked, KNOWING someone was in trouble and you had to get to him/her as quickly as possible?

LOVE SUPERSEDES LOGIC
~ Mr. Scott Visits ~

Poor Mr. Scott.

Thank God he was in a senior's residence that allowed him to share a room with his wife of sixty years. They had been inseparable throughout most of their marriage and living together in residence for the last two years allowed both to be cared for by others when they could no longer care for each other. The 'Missus' was deteriorating quickly, and everyone knew it wouldn't be much longer before she was gone. Everyone was concerned Mr. Scott wouldn't last long after that happened.

Six months had passed since he last held and tenderly kissed his 'Missus' good-bye, and he was surprising us all. Most days he was up and mobile, shuffling down the hall visiting others, sometimes sharing a joke or two. No one had expected him to last this long. I met Mr. Scott while doing volunteer work with the Legion of Mary organization of my church, assisting the priest who served Mass for the residents every Tuesday morning. Everyone fell in LOVE with him on the spot. His shy smile and gentle voice, thanking us for all we were doing melted our hearts. I had only known him a month before Mrs. Scott had passed on and I knew he would need help with wanting to live.

I found out he loved Kentucky Fried Chicken (KFC) and used that to motivate him.

His eyes would twinkle, and he would sit straighter, knowing he was going on a date with the daughter he never had to his favorite restaurant.

This was going to be our fourth outing to KFC.

"I'll pick you up on Saturday morning, Mr. Scott," I said cheerfully, looking forward to our visit as much as he was. He winked and smiled and said he couldn't wait.

Wednesday was uneventful as I went about my chores. We had had other dates but this one felt different. It was the first time he kept popping in my mind frequently. *I wonder if I should call him? What would LOVE do?*

My heart said, "Yes," but my mind said, "No." I knew his slow painful walk up the long hall was stressful, and knowing someone was waiting for him on the phone would make it worse; he would try to rush and cause himself more pain. I also knew some of the staff were easily annoyed and impatient when they had to escort a resident, so I made the logical choice and decided not to call. It would cause too much trouble for everyone. I was going to be seeing him on Saturday anyway, I could wait, so I used logic to talk myself out of it.

Thursday and Friday, he popped into my mind again, *He must be thinking of our date and his KFC,* I convinced myself. Saturday finally arrived.

I dressed up special just for him and went to pick him up. On Tuesdays, I usually entered the side entrance to usher the residents to Mass because it was closer to their rooms.

On this day, I went in the main door announcing I was here to take Mr. Scott on his date.

"I don't think so," a nurse replied curtly. *What's got her knickers in a twist?* I wondered.

"Why," I continued, "does he have visitors?" We had to cancel our second date for that reason; out–of–town friends had arrived unexpectedly.

"We just buried him yesterday," she snapped, appearing very busy and not wanting to deal with me.

"What!" I cried. "You buried him yesterday!" I screamed. "I just saw him Tuesday. We had a luncheon date today. What happened?"

"Are you family?" she asked snootily.

"Family? He doesn't have any family! I'm a friend. Why didn't somebody call me and tell me?"

I was really crying now and really upset! "Why didn't someone call me?"

The nurse informed me, "We are only required to call the next of kin and as you said, you are only a friend. Have a good day," she said and walked away.

I was furious! I ran out the door to my car and just bawled.

If only I had called! If only I had listened to my heart instead of my head.

I kept punishing myself. All of a sudden I knew, *that's why I was thinking about him!* Still, why didn't someone call me? My mind screamed.

"I called," he whispered.

Am I losing my mind? Did I just hear his voice?

Peace and warmth suddenly enveloped me and I knew he was saying good-bye, again.

"Good-bye, my friend," I whispered as I wiped my tears. "I am so sorry I didn't listen better. Thank you for teaching me how."

I realized the one I had been most angry with was myself for being logical. LOVE was letting me know, but I didn't trust. I was still very logical. The peace and warmth Mr. Scott shared with me during his final goodbye enabled me to release my pain and guilt.

When I think of how hard LOVE used him to try and get my attention, I vowed to listen better in the future.

Several times after his last farewell I thought of him and it was always in a similar situation. I knew he was helping me to remember to listen to my heart more than my head. It has been a long while since I have needed him that way, and he still fills my heart with a warm glow whenever I think of him and how important his lesson was.

LOVE certainly did supersede logic.

LOVE ASKS ...

1. Have you ever regret letting your mind's logic overrule your heart?

2. Has someone's spirit try to contact you after that one's death?

3. Would you recognize that one?

*If you can love one
but not the other,
what you have for the one
is not love.*

~ Unknown ~

LOVE POINTS THE WAY
~ I Can't Get Lost ~

Here I was in a strange city to do a presentation; delayed by road construction yet still hoping to make it on time. I came to a T in the road and wasn't sure whether I should turn left or right. My gut was pulling me right, but when I am hungry it sometimes makes a mistake, and I was hungry at this moment.

What would LOVE do? I wondered.

"Turn left," came the reply.

Really? It didn't feel right, but by now I knew to obey. I turned left and went a couple of blocks. My gut was pulling me harder and harder right. *I'll just check with this boy on the sidewalk* I thought.

"Excuse me young man. Can you tell me where St. Paul's School is?"

As soon as I started talking to the boy, the cosmic giggle began inside my belly and I knew why I was told to turn left. In my mind, I could hear the boy's mom telling him not to talk to strangers because he could get into trouble. She wanted to make him street smart through fear; however, his heart was telling him not everyone was bad.

LOVE knew I would ask, listen and obey. It knew It could use me to look lost so the boy could learn to listen and trust his heart.

"You're not too far Ma'am," he said, "you have to go four blocks in the opposite direction."

Exactly where my gut was pulling me to go!

I didn't mind looking lost or being LOVE's fool to be of service. I knew It would always point me in the needed direction

Plus, was I willing to always TRUST LOVE?

I did and still arrive on time!

LOVE ASKS ...

1. How do you teach your children to be street smart?

2. Have you ever experienced hearing a conversation in your head that took place earlier between other people?

3. Do you stop and ask for directions?

LOVE DOES READINGS
~ LOVE Gets The Praise - LOVE Gets The Blame ~

"Do you do readings?" a woman asked me over a cup of coffee at my friend's place.

"No," I replied.

"Will you stop saying no," my friend JoAnna said. "You're always doing readings and you don't even know it!"

Hmmm. I didn't want to do readings, but more than doing what I wanted, I wanted to do what LOVE wanted, so I mentally asked, *What would LOVE do?*

"Say yes next time," came the reply.

Ok LOVE, if you want me to do readings send someone to ask me. I will say yes. If we do well, you get the praise. If we mess up you get the blame, I threatened. *Send me what I need,* I said, quite certain LOVE couldn't be that crazy or desperate!

One week later the phone call came. "Do you do readings?" the caller asked.

Darn it all, I thought. I had to keep my end of the bargain. After a long pause I swallowed hard and replied, "Yes."

"Good, one month from now we are having a spiritual tea and we would like you to participate."

I almost had a heart attack! *A spiritual tea! That is several hours doing many readings! One month would give my old ulcers a lot of time to act up.*

My head was screaming, *No-o-o-o-o!*

"How many hours is the tea?" I asked, trying to sound fearless.

"Four hours," she replied, "with each reading lasting fifteen minutes."

Oh my God! A different person sitting in front of me every fifteen minutes for four hours! I had never even done one!

"Where is it?" I asked, trying to lower my blood pressure. "Peterborough," she replied. *Great, no one knows me. If I blow it I'll just hightail it out of town.* I thought, trying to make light of the panic I was feeling.

If we do well You get the praise. If we mess up, You get the blame. I'll just be the human telephone. I kept thinking to myself over and over again. Obviously, LOVE wanted to know how I would handle this; if I would trust that all would be Ok.

Every time I thought of the tea, I would repeat, *If we do well, You get the praise. If we mess up, You get the blame! Send me what I need.* Peace and calmness would enter my body and I would totally forget about the tea.

It was time. I was sitting on my chair, feeling amazingly calm.

The first customer sat down and introduced herself in her prim and proper British accent.

Oh shoot, she's British! They're into all this kind of stuff and can spot a phony a mile away.

"Do you have a ring or watch I could hold for a moment," I asked trying to sound like I knew what I was doing.

"Oh, you use psychometry," she commented delightfully. *Blimey, she knows what the word means! Most people haven't even heard the word. I just learned about it myself!*

"Oh, you know about psychometry?" I asked, trying to look unaffected.

She then proceeded to tell me about all the classes she had studied in Britain and the names of the famous people she had had readings with; people I had heard and read about. *Oh, my God!* I thought. *No! You get the praise. You get the blame. You set me up. You'd better help! It's all in Your hands.*

I held her watch and began speaking. Within two sentences she was crying. I continued till the bell rang, signaling it was time to end our session.

"I wish you lived where I lived," she said as she got up.

"Why?" I asked.

"I would take classes from you," she replied.

Classes! Is she crazy? "Where do you live?" I asked, praying it was a million miles away. *I am no teacher! I don't even know what I am doing here!*

"I live in Gananoque," she replied. It was a fifteen-minute drive from my house in Kingston, Ontario!

Guess who was my first student; this brave, trusting, wonderful woman. At the end of the eight-week class she approached me saying, "You know that reading you did for me in Peterborough?"

"Yes," I said.

"Everything you said came true right to the date my son would have his experience."

"I gave you dates?" I asked, surprised. Dates were a hard thing to be accurate about, when dealing with the spiritual world, because there is no such thing as time on the other side. I couldn't remember anything I had told her! I later realized that that would be normal for me because I usually went into an altered state and was often unaware of what had transpired.

That spiritual tea was the first time I officially did readings, but it wouldn't be the last. I soon began to realize what JoAnna meant when she said I was always doing readings and didn't even know it. It was very easy for me to become one with someone and know them in a way they often didn't know themselves. I realized LOVE wanted me to serve in this way so I decided I had better learn a thing or two. Psychometry was the first technique I studied, then rune stones, numerology, tarot cards, crystals and whatever else LOVE sent my way.

A few years later, someone asked me to do a reading and I replied, "Sorry, I don't have my cards with me."

The look on her face made me feel that I really needed to help her, so I did my usual and asked, *What would LOVE do?*

"What would the Master have done? Did he have a bag of goodies?" came the reply.

No, he didn't. From that moment on I have not used a single thing. I just sit with the person, say my opening prayer and watch what my body feels and does. I immediately begin to feel the person's pain, issues, attitude, whatever I need to know and I let LOVE guide me.

I remember telling LOVE, "If we do well, LOVE gets the praise. If we mess up, you get the blame." LOVE hasn't failed me yet.

The power of LOVE still amazes me! If It wants you to do something, It will send you everything you need, all you have to do is ask and trust.

LOVE ASKS ...

1. Do you think you could do readings?

2. Why do you think I felt I needed to study many ways to do readings if I was already doing them?

3. Why don't you hold something that belongs to someone else and see what pictures, feelings, thoughts come to your mind?

LOVE is wisdom,
LOVE is in giving,
LOVE is God and God is LOVE,
but there is no wise or fools for LOVE.

LOVE
is equal for each one of us.

~ Santosh Kalwar ~
https://www.goodreads.com/author/quotes/2894169.Santosh_Kalwar

LOVE IS DIVINE ORDER
~ Religion vs. Spirituality ~

"Let there be divine order in this situation," JoAnna would say whenever she found herself in a pickle - losing her car keys, being stuck in traffic, or being late for something - and it seemed to make things better. Whenever some cruelty occurred, she would repeat, "All is in divine order." She made it sound like it was ok!

How could it be ok to rape, murder, or rob someone? She was driving me crazy with this divine order stuff. *What was she talking about?* No matter how Jo and her husband Barry tried to explain it to me, it just didn't register.

I had just spent sixteen years in the military, I knew what order was! The rules and regulations were exact; there was to be no bending of the rules, or any discussion to be had about them.

The divine to me meant God, the Church, religion, and most of them had tons of rules and dogmas. When I compared religions, looking for the right one, all I saw was their differences till LOVE inspired me to look for their similarities. Bingo! They were all basically saying the same thing. There is only one God and many different religions, all expressing God the way they understood God to be.

Still, I couldn't understand this divine order way of being. LOVE knew I had to work it out for myself.

Many years of questioning, searching, and experiencing began clarifying divine order for me.

As strange as it seemed, I had to separate religion from God to know more. Many readers would consider that statement a ticket to hell.

If you are one of these, I ask you to look at the differences between them.

Religion's answers never varied; whereas, every time I asked, "What would LOVE do?" I got an answer that was different yet perfect for each situation. I was never taught to think that way in Church.

RELIGION	SPIRITUALITY
• Separate us: theirs vs. ours	♥ Unites us: We are One
• Uses fear	♥ Divine LOVE casts out fear
• Many dogmas and decrees Do's and don'ts or else	♥ Two simple requests LOVE God and others
• Same for everyone	♥ Likes Variety – Empowers
• Challenges free thinking	♥ Encourages free thinking
• God is outside self	♥ Is inside everyone
• Scripture hard to understand	♥ Language/simple
• Speaks thru ordained	♥ Speaks directly to all
• All is right or wrong	♥ Paradoxical
• Love is conditional	♥ LOVE is unconditional

I began to understand that every time I asked for divine order in my feelings, decisions or situations, I was making a freewill statement requesting alignment of my will with the universal - divine, **LOVE's** will, which always gave me exactly what I needed, when, if, and how I needed it, every time.

LOVE, divine order, quickly transformed my fear into courage, anger into peace, fatigue into energy, and confusion into clarity.

If I asked for divine order in a terrible situation, essentially, I was asking, that whatever was unfolding, be supported, played out, allowed, in the

easiest, quickest way, that was in the greatest interest of all concerned, and according to the bigger picture

The violent acts that used to confuse me were now seen as perfect opportunities for the 'victim' to demonstrate the power of divine order/**LOVE**.

If someone came here to show the power of **LOVE** through forgiveness … there had to be someone to forgive!

Orders can be interpreted as laws.

For example, when I was in pain (in this case experiencing a human law that said a broken bone hurts and would take so many weeks to heal); asking for divine order in my body reconnected me to a greater truth, a more powerful law which states …

I AM SPIRIT
NOTHING
CAN HURT ME OR MAKE ME SICK OR AFRAID
WHY?
BECAUSE SPIRIT IS GOD
GOD
CANNOT BE SICK, HURT OR AFRAID!
I HAVE COME HERE TO PROVE THAT
THROUGH THIS BODY
NOW!

Remembering that I am a spiritual being having a human experience (and not a human trying to become spiritual) caused me to heal in what some would call miraculous time!

It only seems a miracle because we have forgotten the greater truths and laws. Trying to understand divine order led me to finally remember we are magnificent beings of light, here to do LOVE's work, to be LOVE in action, to represent the Creator because the Creator cannot be manifest on this planet in Its full form.

It is too powerful; it would be like a million watts going through a 20-watt bulb! The light bulb would explode. The Creator, LOVE, sent little parts of it, you and me, to do its work. We are chips off the old block!

As spiritual beings we would be invisible, angel-like, to most humans.

To help us do our work we were given a space suit that would makes us visible; that space suit is called a body and it is the most valuable thing we possess.

LOVE sent JoAnna and Barry to introduce me to a new way of thinking, being, and remembering. Asking LOVE to help me understand it all transformed me from a confused, frightened, angry, human into a wiser, more courageous, spiritual being remembering her mission ... to be LOVE in action.

Thank you JoAnna and Barry for your patience. All is in divine order!

LOVE ASKS ...

1. Which is true for you?

> a. You are a human trying to become spiritual.
> b. You are a spiritual being having a human experience.
> c. You don't have a clue!

2. Are you willing to align your will with LOVE's will?

3. Will you try to remember who you really are?

4000 years ago, leaders said,
"I am your leader, follow me"
and they led us into war.

2000 year ago, leaders said,
"I am your leader, I will teach you"
and they taught us
what they wanted us to know.

Today's wise leaders say,
"I am your leader,
how may I serve you?"

~ Lance Secretan ~
http://www.imdb.com/name/nm0781200/bio

LOVE SHOWS CHARLENE DIVINE ORDER
~ LOVE Is More Powerful Than A Curse ~

"Yes Caroline, everything is in divine order, Caroline. Yes Caroline, everything is in f- -king divine order!" Charlene yelled at the top of her lungs. She was furious!

Four days earlier, Charlene had reminded her husband, "I won't be back until very late Friday night Ron. Don't forget we have that doctor's appointment in Toronto Saturday and we must leave here by 5 a.m. The car won't make the three-hour journey each way as it is, so make sure you take it in to get checked."

"No problem," Ron replied. He was now retired and knew he would have time to look into it.

Charlene got home around 11 p.m. Friday evening and after the welcome home hugs and kisses she asked Ron how much work had to be done on the car. Guess who had completely forgotten! Ron was in real trouble and Charlene was extremely angry. They'd waited over six months for this appointment. It was too late to repair the car now. The trip would have to be cancelled.

Thank God for water! Whenever she was stressed, Charlene would take a long bath, and fully submerge herself under the bubbles. The water always relieved her stress whatever the cause. This night it was going to have to work overtime.

"What would LOVE do?" she thought angrily. She then remembered a class where I had told her and the others about divine order.

"Yes Caroline, everything is in divine order Caroline, Yes Caroline, everything is in effin divine order," she continued yelling out loud, not caring who heard. She must have repeated it about seven times when suddenly she became quiet and then exploded in laughter. "Yes, Caroline. Everything IS in divine order!"

Cursing while asking for divine order had not stopped LOVE from helping Charlene. It reminded her of her mother-in-law's big luxury car across the street and her recent request for someone to take it for a long spin because she hadn't used it in months.

Charlene couldn't stop laughing as she called to tell me how angry she had been with me, divine order, her husband, the doctor, and the whole world.

"I sure am glad LOVE listened to my heart and not my cursing," she said. "I was amazed at how quickly it worked! I never believed you when you told us about it but now I know for myself. I will trust you more and I will certainly trust divine order!"

Charlene and her family drove in luxury that Saturday enjoying something her car did not have, air conditioning, on that record breaking hot day!

Wasn't it perfect that Ron had forgotten to get the car fixed? Did LOVE move him to forget? Did Charlene need to have her own knowing of divine order and how quickly and easily it worked?

If Ron had had the car fixed they would have used it and would not have enjoyed the air-conditioner LOVE knew they would need.

My mind is very visual and, to this day, I can still see Charlene sputtering and spitting in her bubble bath, creating more bubbles with her temper tantrum while LOVE just watched and waited for her energy to shift.

The look on her face must have been priceless!

"Yes Caroline, everything is in divine order."

LOVE ASKS ...

1. Have you forgotten to do something only to later find out it was not necessary in the end?

2. What do you do to shift from anger to peace?

3. Does cursing seem to help you?

*A truly strong person
does not need the approval of others
any more than
a lion needs the approval of sheep.*

~ Vernon Howard ~
http://www.anewlife.org/About/Vernon_Howard/vernon_howard.html

LOVE STARTS A NEW GAME
~ Time To Meet New Teachers ~

On the 15th of May of 1989 I began playing a little game asking, "If it was my last week alive and I could do only one thing, what would I really really really want to do?"

I thought skydiving would come to mind because I've always wanted to experience flying through the air. Loud and clear I heard, "Go swim with dolphins."

I don't think so! my mind screamed. *I've almost drowned three times! I hate the water! I've heard of the movie Flipper but I haven't even seen a picture of a dolphin! I am scared out of my skin. I don't want to swim with dolphins! NO! NO! NO!* I mentally screamed! *Ok, calm down. Let's just pretend we're swimming with dolphins, what would happen?* I asked myself.

In my imagination a dolphin appeared and filled me with LOVE. I began crying and shaking so much I thought I was going to levitate. *Time out!* I thought. *Somebody wants me to go swim with dolphins. I don't know who, I don't know where, I don't know why and it probably costs a zillion dollars.*

By now I was really panicking and could hardly breathe. *What would LOVE do?* I half-heartedly asked.

"Go swim with dolphins," I heard.

I was not impressed. This LOVE stuff sure ticked me off at times.

Ok! I'll go swim with dolphins but you had better send me what I need; the opportunity, the place, the money, and most of all the courage and ability, I mentally screamed.

Within two weeks I had news from Russia, Hawaii, Florida, TV, newspapers, and magazines. Everywhere I looked I was staring a dolphin in the face and I had not even seen a picture of these 'fish' before.

Key Largo, Florida, in November was better than Kingston, Ontario, Canada where I lived at the time. There was a five-day course swimming, playing, and meditating with them.

I phoned and was told I could not go. "We have fourteen on the course and thirty on the waiting list."

"Put my name down, I am going," I replied.

"You sound so sure. How do you know?"

"The universe does not give me the desire to do something and then shut the door in my face," I answered. "It doesn't work that way."

I just heard, "Oh? Ok," at the other end of the line.

One week later the young lady called me back saying, "One person on the course cancelled. The other thirty cannot make it; do you still want to swim with dolphins?"

I started to shake and vibrate again. *Oh, my God! Thirty-one people were moved aside so I could swim with dolphins. Somebody really wants me to go!*

I now knew they weren't fish. I now knew how big and fast they were and that they saved people from drowning.

They are going to have to save me because I am going to drown for sure. Somebody wants me to die ... to have a near death experience.

I asked, "What do I have to do to survive this ordeal?"

"You must tread water in deep salt water for half an hour with mask, snorkel, and fins."

Dear God! Don't you ever give me a break? I've done five minutes treading water, pulled a groin muscle and needed months of therapy. Mask and snorkel make me claustrophobic. Again, I was panicking. *Send me what I need. I will do it!* I wailed, absolutely petrified.

Two weeks later my nephew was visiting and said, "Let's go swimming, Auntie."

I had to get into the water sooner or later. *If you want me to tread water for half an hour you had better take over my legs because I can't do this by myself,* I demanded. I was almost in tears. *At least there's a lifeguard here who can save me if I start going down.*

I spent two hours in the deep end of the pool like a water polo expert. It was no effort whatsoever!

That was the only time I was in the water before November. I swam with them and they changed my life forever.

They continue to do so many years later. In the big scheme of things one thing leads to another.

Sometime later I played my one-week-alive game again and was told, "Have a newspaper column sharing the things you teach in class."

Yea! Right. They're going to burn me at the stake as a witch. I gave in. *Ok! Ok! Send me what I need, again.*

One half hour later, my next client arrived. She was thrilled with her session and when it came time for her to pay me she me took my breath away. In those days I did not set a fee for my services; I accepted LOVE offerings. Each client was told to ask, "What would LOVE leave Caroline for our time together?" and they had to do what their heart told them. That's how I got my TV, computer, books, jewelry, haircuts, trip to Hawaii, dog kennels cleaned, and so forth. Sometimes I even got money.

"I am not supposed to give you money," my client said. "I am to offer you my service. I own a newspaper. Would you be interested in having a column teaching what you do?"

Whoopee! I cheered internally. *Oh, geez. How can I do this and remain anonymous?* I prayed and meditated, got five ideas for the title and put them in a hat.

I then asked, *What does LOVE want to call this column?* I drew out one idea and threw it back in and tried again.

Time after time I kept drawing out the same title. I didn't think it was so great but when my husband drew the same title I gave in. I suddenly realized why it was so perfect!

Readers could take the information as fact or fantasy and I could remain anonymous.

The new column was called DOLPHIN TEACHINGS. The dolphins would appear each week and teach about meditation, powers of colors, sound, mental telepathy, and more. It was perfect.

It must have been, because it was the first time the newspaper had received a letter from a subscriber complimenting them on their new column.

That column has since become a book called DOLPHIN WHISPERS. Once again, LOVE used my weakness to show its strength in this new and very challenging game while introducing me to some very powerful and wise teachers.

LOVES ASKS ...

1. Have you ever been in the water with dolphins?

2. Did you know dolphins know within 48 hrs of conception if a woman is pregnant?

3. Did you know they will LOVE you and spend time with you as much as you LOVE and spend time with yourself? They give you what you need, not what you want. What do you think the dolphins want you to know?

LOVE LOWERS ME TO RAISE OTHERS
~ Tough LOVE In Action ~

I was working for a week with a full schedule counseling depressed, angry, frightened, searching souls for eight hours a day, every day for six days. My hosts were a couple who offered their home to lessen my expenses. I looked forward to a place where I could relax, recharge my batteries, have peace and view a beautiful lake. I would leave their home in the morning, do my work, and return in time for supper.

Three days had passed and every evening their heated arguments, cursing and threats began; creating a great deal of stress that left me completely exhausted and drained. I tried being the minister, the spiritual advisor and friend. I tried every technique I knew, including prayer. Nothing seemed to make a difference, to register or to stick. I was working miracles with my clients but couldn't get to first base with this couple.

The fourth day of work had been quite hectic, dealing with a family that had lost a son to suicide, a school presentation on anger management, and others seeking their life's purpose. When my day was done, I wondered what mood I would be met with when I reached my hosts' home.

Things had not changed. The familiar chill was in the air. You could have cut the tension with a knife. The table was set for dinner.

We were all seated and it began in full force. He kept threatening suicide; maybe he would kill her first. On and on it went.

Inside I was screaming, *What can I do? I've tried everything I know!*

"Have you tried your Magical Question?" LOVE asked.

No sooner had I thought, *What would LOVE do?* I found myself pounding both fists on the table as I stood up. The dishes thumped up and down and I yelled, "I've had enough of this f - - king horse s - - t! If you two want to kill each other, be my guests.

"I work hard all day in a stressful environment and need to have a place where there is peace. I am grateful you tried to save me some money but you have caused me more stress than it is worth. I have tried to help you in every way I know, I can't do any more. I am getting my things and moving to a hotel. I don't need this horsesh* t anymore! I'm outta here!"

I had never said that 'F' word before. I felt possessed! The strangest thing happened while I was acting like a crazy person on the outside; I had a deep stillness inside me that felt so solid nothing could disturb it.

I started to leave and both yelled, "Stop! We don't want you to go." They each apologized to me, looked at each other and began talking.

I stood there in awe! I had tried the kind, spiritual stuff and nothing worked. I cursed, and was nasty and they responded! I stayed. They talked all night long. All of us grew. It was the only way to connect with them so they would hear me.

I have since learned that when Caroline is acting upset on the outside and feels upset inside, it is Caroline's stuff surfacing, needing attention.

However, when Caroline acts upset on the outside and is very still and calm on the inside, LOVE is using her to act angrily to get their attention, to make a difference, to change things.

LOVE isn't always beautiful, soft, and nice. Even Jesus had moments of anger, and turned tables over. If it was good enough for Him, it was certainly good enough for me.

LOVE lowered me so it could pick them up and raise them closer to each other.

LOVE ASKS ...

1. Have you ever acted out of character and wondered what the heck was happening?

2. Do you now see why your words, advice and attempts to change others do not always work?

3. Did you know that the language you use reveals the level of your intelligence?

It is the mark of an educated mind to be able to entertain a thought without accepting it.

~ Aristotle ~
https://www.biography.com/people/aristotle-9188415

LOVE'S BIRTHDAY WISH
~ Why You Are So Important ~

During my first dolphin swim, I remembered that I would be missing the birthdays of several dear friends and family. Every time I bought a birthday card I made a point of adding a few notes to remind them how special their birth was in the big scheme of things.

Shirley MacLaine (the actress in Out On A Limb) once wrote that all our guides and angels gather around for twenty-four-hours during our birth – 12 hours before and 12 hours after. She suggested we go into nature during that time to be silent and to decide what we want to manifest the following year. She added our guides and angels would help us make it happen, if it was part of our divine plan.

I was beginning to realize I would have a lot of writing to do when I got home and would probably end up with writer's cramp, which I often got because of breaking both my wrists more than once.

I was thinking of the cards when one of the dolphins swam by, nudged me and seemed to giggle; their clicking sounds often made me think they were laughing at me for being so serious at times. Spock, the genius dolphin, looked me in the eye and I immediately got the thought, *Create your own card!*

Wow! Great idea! One week later I was home sitting at my desk wondering what to write for my birthday card.

I wondered *What would LOVE write?* and a wonderful 20-line poem unfolded in about five minutes.

I printed it onto some fancy art paper and framed it. It was beautiful. I also energize it with some techniques I've learned in the past.

It became one of the best birthday presents I ever gave because it told each person why he or she is so special to the Creator and to human-kind.

I was inspired to insert the birthday person's name in beautiful calligraphy.

I will share the poem for you to read.

When personalizing it for buyers, I add the name of their loved one at the appropriate place.

ORIGIN OF THE BIRTHDAY WISH

LONG LONG AGO, LONG BEFORE TIME BEGAIN
GOD MADE THE EARTH
AS PART OF HIS GREATER PLAN
GOD SAID ...

I want to laugh and sing, to create wonderful things
To share the peace and joy My total LOVE brings.

I created Earth in such a wondrous way
That to be, has to be done in a very special way.

To feel and to know I will have a shape and form
Through a physical body is the way I will be born.

There's joyous celebration each time I arrive
The birth of a new babe is proof that I'm alive!

A twinkling part of Me volunteered to be
Born in human form so I could be known as Thee

John

I've sent You guides and angels
To remind You of your light
So We can be together,
Our light will shine so bright!

My dear and wondrous child,
it's through You that I'm alive
Together We will be …We will play …
We will strive.

Because You are so special, helping Me to be
I give You a Birthday Wish …
As You think …it shall be!

On this Our special day,
And on this day each year hence
Whatever is Your wish,
My command is that it's sent.

Yes, My precious child, I give My thanks to You
Give thought to Your wish,
Guides and angels make it true!

Your body is My vehicle transporting Me to Earth
All the gold and all the treasures
Cannot match what It is worth!

It has become a tradition of mine to frame it and gift
it to the parents of a newborn child.

It is also one of my most enjoyed birthday gifts.

I have whispered it in the ear of a child in intensive care and have always been amazed at the feeling of peace and healing that comes over everyone in the room, especially the child.

I remember quietly saying it to a hospitalized fifty-eight-year-old friend who was being monitored from head to toe. He was in a coma and when I finished the poem a nurse came into the room to see what was happening because his readings had suddenly changed for the better. He squeezed my hand to let me know he had heard and began to make a quick recovery. LOVE used Spock to inspire me to write this poem.

It is presently available as a frameable scroll with a variety of backgrounds dependent upon the age of the recipient.

LOVE ASKS ...

1. Have you ever made a birthday wish that came true?

2. Would you now consider spending 24 hours, 12 hours before and 12 hours after your birth time, in nature to decide what you want to manifest for the next year?

3. Do you know why I used upper case, capitals for You, Our, We?

LOVE CONQUERS FEAR
~ Holding The Perfection ~

It was eleven thirty on a Thursday night, quite late for a phone call. *Wonder who's calling at this hour?*

"We need your help!" whispered the woman hoarsely. "Things are happening in our house and we can't stop them."

"What kind of things?" I asked.

"Doors are opening and shutting by themselves. Things are crashing to the floor and I can feel an evil presence!"

Her fear was coming through the phone line and touching me. *I must be ready to handle this or LOVE would not send it to me!* I tried to convince myself. *Everyone concerned, including me, is protected. Nothing but goodness can come to me, to us!* I seriously considered rejecting her cry for help but when I asked my Magical Question, *What would LOVE do?* I heard, "Go and do your YOU ARE routine."

That didn't make me feel any braver. *Send me what I need, protection, wisdom, courage, everything P-L-E-A-S-E!* I mentally pleaded.

I talked to the woman a little longer, to calm her and myself down and then said, "I'll see you tomorrow morning at nine o'clock." I didn't want to go into any haunted house at midnight.

"Do we need silver candlesticks?" the woman questioned.

"Silver candlesticks? No. I just need the people involved," I answered, puzzled by the question.

Needless to say, I did not sleep well that night; actually, I did not sleep at all. Every horror movie I had ever seen replayed itself in my mind.

STOP! I am protected! LOVE would never send me anything I can't handle. It would never want to hurt me. It wants to use me to help others.

It was now time to get ready to go. *What shall I wear?* I wondered.

Running shoes, blue jeans, and a sweatshirt, popped into my mind. *That's not very professional,* I argued. *Running shoes, blue jeans, and a sweatshirt. Running shoes, blue jeans, and a sweatshirt. Ok! Ok! Who really cares what I am wearing anyway!*

I dressed and hesitantly made my way over to the haunted home. I sat outside the hi-rise apartment building wondering what I was getting myself into.

All the horror movies I have seen had ghosts in houses, not apartment buildings. LOVE certainly had a funny sense of humor.

Oh, well, here goes. Give me what I need! were the only thoughts I had as I entered the building and knocked on apartment 802.

I was escorted into an apartment that was filled with beer bottles, dirty dishes, food, clothing, and cigarette butts everywhere.

Where does one sit in this place?

A place was cleared for me at the kitchen table. A woman, her child, and her boyfriend lived there with two other adult females present. One woman had six bibles piled up on the kitchen table with her hands in a praying position over them. As soon as I sat down she yelled, "I'll have you know I am a Christian!"

"Good, so am I," I replied, not adding that I studied all the other religions as well.

"Oh," she mumbled.

The mother loudly told her five-year-old daughter to go to her room or to go across the hall to her friend's place. The little girl began throwing a temper tantrum. Throughout all the yelling and fussing, I was getting the gut feeling that it was not an uneasy spirit causing things to fly around.

Someone was so full of anger that it was coming out of his or her gut, hitting things and sending them flying. I had heard three people and each of them could have been the cause. I didn't think they raised their voices because someone was deaf.

It definitely felt like anger.

I asked the mother, "Do you mind if your daughter sits on my lap for a few minutes?"

She replied loudly, "She doesn't go to strangers but if you call her name and she comes, Ok." Her name was Judy.

"Judy, bring your coloring book and crayons and come sit on my lap for a few minutes."

She immediately did so. I then asked her to, "Color a picture in your coloring book and tell me a long story about the picture you are coloring."

I wanted her talking while I was doing my YOU ARE routine. I had been doing this YOU ARE routine for years. I never knew why I began it or where it came from but it felt like I had to do it.

In my mind I was thinking,

Judy,
You are a perfect manifestation of God.
You are a child of light.

You are Spirit.
Nothing can hurt you or make you sick or afraid.

Why?

Because Spirit is God.
God cannot be sick, hurt or afraid.

In those days, if I touched people, I would pick up their vibrations, their energy. If they had a bad back I would then have a bad back. If they spoke with an accent I would begin speaking with an accent. There were times when I was afraid people would think

I was mocking or making fun of them, eventually I learned to trust what was happening.

As I had one hand on Judy's chest and the other on her back, sandwiching her heart and lungs, I suddenly wanted to vomit all kinds of phlegm and mucus. As my body reacted to hers, I began thinking …

Judy,
You are perfect health.
You are joy. You are peace.
No matter what your human body
looks like or acts out,
you are perfection.
Manifest your true self through your body
NOW!

Her human body was the one throwing a temper tantrum, acting sick, but the real her, spirit, was absolute perfection.

I kept thinking these thoughts over and over until I heard, "Enough" in my mind. I then sent her across the hall to her friend's place. Before leaving she insisted on giving me a nice long hug.

I then spent the next two hours educating the adults about energy.

Little Judy then returned to get ready for kindergarten. Without being asked, she immediately sat on my lap and ate her grilled cheese sandwich. I mentally repeated my YOU ARE routine.

When it was time to catch the bus, she gave me several hugs and gave everyone else in the room a hug. Everyone looked a little puzzled.

I couldn't see why hugging family caused confusion. The woman with the bibles, her aunt, walked Judy to the elevator to catch the bus. She returned to the apartment and immediately yelled at me, "What did you do to that child?"

"I don't understand," I replied.

The aunt proceeded to tell me that Judy had cystic fibrosis and was recovering from double pneumonia.

She said she had been trying to get Judy to say the word LOVE for many years and all Judy would do is run around the apartment saying, "I hate you! I hate you!"

That's when my light came on!

It was Judy who was causing things to fly around. The cigarette smoke, poor food, negative surroundings, and poor care were making her sick. She didn't know how to express her anger any other way. It was unconsciously coming out of her solar plexus, (where one gets butterfly feelings) hitting things and sending them flying.

"What happened?" I asked, totally puzzled.

"I was walking her down the hall to catch the bus and I asked her out of curiosity, 'Do you like that woman that's visiting?"

"Like that woman? I LOVE that woman!" was Judy's reply.

There was that word LOVE!

"You LOVE that woman? Why do you LOVE that woman?" the aunt questioned confused.

Judy's reply brought a tear to my eye and shivers up my spine.

"I LOVE that woman because she talked to me in my heart!"

I now knew why I had been sent there. I had to know my YOU ARE routine made a difference. She heard every single thought! It worked!

All those years thinking it in grocery stores, in banks, on the highway, in the malls, everywhere, were worth the effort.

I explained that they could do the same as I and even more.

The aunt then said something else I needed to hear. "You know when you walked in wearing running shoes, blue jeans, and a sweatshirt I heaved a sigh of relief."

"Why?" I asked.

"The woman who gave us your name is a witch. We thought you were a witch too. We thought you would be wearing a long black dress. When you came in dressed as you were, I saw you were normal like the rest of us. That's why we asked if we needed silver candlesticks."

Again, I was blown away! My favorite thing to wear was an ankle length, long-sleeve, turtle necked, black dress with boots and a vest.

LOVE is the greatest power ... It cancels all fear. LOVE tested me. Did I LOVE enough to possibly sacrifice my life to go into a haunted house? Would I trust that I would be given everything I need to accomplish the task at hand? Would I wear what I was told? Plus, the biggie ... the YOU ARE routine made a difference! It worked! It was real, solid!

A few months later Judy's aunt phoned to tell me that they had fantastic news. Judy's lungs were completely clear of pneumonia and she no longer had cystic fibrosis plus she had not sent things flying once since my visit. They had all begun to send her thoughts as I had done. I suppose we all needed to go through the experience to learn the power of thoughts and about thinking and speaking the truth.

Each of us is perfect spirit inside these human bodies, acting out illness as required for our soul's purpose; and when our soul is reminded of LOVE's truth, miracles happen. Are they really miracles or just rememberings?

LOVE ASKS ...

1. Have you ever experienced angry energy being sent to you by others?

2. Have you ever been in a haunted house or felt the presence of spirit in your home?

3. Do you now realize how you can help someone who is sick, afraid, angry, experiencing lack?

Life's Priorities

1. *The God of your understanding.*
2. *Your God Self, your life's purpose.*
4. *Your spouse.*
5. *Your children*
6. *Your job.*
7. *Your extended family.*
8. *Your community*

*Put them in that order
and you'll never make a mistake.*

~ Unity Church ~
https://en.wikipedia.org/wiki/Unity_Church

LOVE CHOOSES LOVE
~ Cancer Is Healed ~

"You don't have much time left," the doctor said hesitantly. "It would be best to put your house in order."

A loud *NO!* pierced Jane's head. *I'm not ready to die! I'm too young!* She was told it would be a few months at the most. Jane had undergone several surgeries to repair the twenty-one holes in her abdomen. The doctors would suture the holes and the sutures would rot and fester. Cancer was slowly eating her alive.

Jane believed in reincarnation and came for a past life regression on November 8th, 1982. It was a day I will never forget. She was so pale and weak and had the unusual ability of being able to see inside bodies. She told me how ugly hers looked, but worse, was how it felt.

Once she was comfortably settled on my massage table, we began. I said my opening prayer and asked our guides and angels to take us back in time to where the seed of this cancer was first planted.

Jane went back in time to where the soul wanted the human personality to master forgiveness.

How?

LOVE led her back to a time when Jane was male, black, in the southern states when the Klu Klux Klan was everywhere.

Would there be any chances to practice forgiveness? Many.

"Back of the bus, nigger. You can't eat here. You can't go there" and on and on it went. Boy, as Jane was called then, experienced every degradation and insult a black person could experience at the hands of white people.

Boy's life ended quite young, tied to a stake with all the Klansmen around.

All he could see were the eyes of the white man who held the three-pronged pitchfork. Seven times the fork went in and out of Boy's abdomen.

Each time his mind screamed, "I HATE YOU! I HATE YOU! I HATE YOU! I HATE WHITES! I WANT TO KILL YOU!"

Boy died hating whites. He left his body; went through the tunnel towards the light and began his life review. He needed to see if he had fulfilled his life's mission. It was time to remember everything.

- ♥ He relived every opportunity he had had to demonstrate forgiveness and saw how he kept choosing to hate.
- ♥ He remembered the power of the color purple; that blue/violet color, the hottest part of the flame that changes ice into water then into steam; the color that changes anger into LOVE, fear into courage, negative into positive, slow moving energy into faster and more powerful energy; and saw how he kept choosing the murky red of anger.

- ♥ He remembered the power of LOVE; remembered how LOVE causes a brain to create endorphins giving the body a 'high' that makes it impossible to feel pain, fear or anger and saw how he continued to choose hate.

- ♥ He remembered if he came to demonstrate and master forgiveness, there had to be someone to forgive, a bad guy.

- ♥ He remembered that the bad guy is often someone who loves you so much from another lifetime, he volunteers to be your bad guy, knowing you would hate him, yet loved you so much he volunteered to be your bad guy so you could become a master.

- ♥ He remembered causing someone pain and was experiencing what that felt like for that person, because he was now experiencing it as though it was his own.

- ♥ He remembered it was impossible to hurt someone unless that person's soul, at some level, gave permission for the experience - to practice forgiveness, to repay a karmic debt, to remember how to get out of a body, to allow others to judge or not, or any other of the many reasons one can have for choosing to experience pain.

- ♥ He remembered, I AM SPIRIT Perfect ... Holy ... Harmonious Nothing can hurt me or make me sick or afraid. Why? Because Spirit is God. God cannot be sick hurt or afraid. I am to manifest my true self through this body NOW!"

- ♥ No matter what my physical body looks like or acts out I AM SPIRIT ... I AM PERFECTION!
- ♥ He remembered everything and experienced everything from every angle possible.

Oh God! I blew it! I forgot! Boy kept crying over and over.

That's when LOVE told him, "No problem, My child, go and try again."

Boy came back as Jane.

Remember whatever you die with ... you come back with!

Jane now knew why she hated looking at herself in the mirror ... she was white! She now knew why she had a passion for black music, black food, black people. She used to be black!

She now knew why, the minute she made eye contact with the white man, wearing a mask at a Halloween party, the words, *I hate you! I hate you! I hate you! I hate whites! I want to kill you!* surfaced out of her deep sub-conscious memory.

She did not consciously remember Boy's past life but the memory was in her DNA. Her cells remembered. Jane thought, *I really don't like or trust whites but why do I hate this one?*

That's when the cancer began eating holes in her abdomen, twenty-one to be exact.

He had been the Klu Klux Klan member with the three-pronged pitchfork.

Believe it or not, they got married and were constantly at each other's throats, arguing and name calling.

Jane asked, "Why would two souls who hate each other choose to get married?"

It was simple to explain.

"If you came to master unconditional LOVE with a particular person, and you two were just casual acquaintances, you could tell each other to get lost, to get out of your life. But get married! You will have to work at it twenty-four hours a day, every day of the week! It could kill you or cure you. It's easy to LOVE someone who is kind; however, a Master wants to be able to LOVE anyone, everyone.

Think of it, how many people get married and don't REALLY LOVE each other?"

I continued, "You wanted to Master loving others and he wanted to master loving himself.

You have been lovers in other lifetimes, making it so easy for you to get emotionally involved. You both loved each other so much, you volunteered to get together, to marry, and to support each other in your soul's master lessons."

Well, they did get married and almost killed each other. Hate was slowly killing her again. It was time for Jane to go back to Boy's original death scene.

This time he had Jane's experience to help him make wiser choices.

This time Boy thought, *Thank you. Thank you. Thank you. Because of you I am becoming more Godlike, more forgiving. I release you. You don't have to be my bad guy anymore. Go and be the perfect LOVE you were destined to be.*

Thank you for giving me the opportunity to experience unconditional LOVE!

Healing tears were flowing down Jane's cheeks, she then looked me in the eyes and said, "Finish it for me."

I had no idea what she was talking about. After a short pause, I took a deep breath and asked, *What would LOVE do?* I found myself gently putting my hands over her abdomen and Holding the Perfection. I kept reminding the cells in her body of their perfection, no matter how things looked on the outside … they were absolute perfection.

I continued for about five minutes when suddenly Jane whispered shakily, "It's happening! The holes are closing!"

In that 1½ hour session LOVE healed and closed the door on the past and the holes in her body. The doctors never admitted the possibility of a wonderful healing and she didn't care. She and her former husband became friends again, and that was all that mattered.

Jane did die, but not of cancer ... the cancer was gone. She did die ... twenty years later of a street drug overdose.

I often wondered why she never returned to work on her other issues. Maybe LOVE sent her to me to remind me of the power of choosing LOVE over hate.

She demonstrated the power of LOVE to forgive others. Maybe now she is working on forgiving herself.

This story was not shared to prove the existence of past lives. That belief makes no difference to LOVE or me. The choices are what is important. Allow LOVE to choose and it will always choose what is in the highest interest of all concerned. I didn't do anything anyone else could not do ... all I did was LOVE and let LOVE come through to inspire my words and actions to help Jane make a new and higher choice for all concerned.

LOVE ASKS ...

1. Is there someone you are choosing to continue hating, not forgiving?

2. Do you believe in past lives, reincarnation? Could that explain why you immediately distrust or LOVE someone?

3. Would you be willing to let LOVE move you to understand more?

You do not have the luxury of being nervous right now!

Someone needs your help.

*You are here to serve ...
serve the best you can.*

*If you cannot help,
direct the person to someone who can.*

*If you want
to get sick to your stomach afterward,
be my guest.*

*You do not have that luxury
right now!*

~ Margaret Kean ~
Master Teacher ~ Had 3 Near Death Experiences
Didn't come back the 4th time.

LOVE STOPS SUICIDE'S SEDUCTION
~ To Be Or Not To Be ...That Is The Question ~

Her father, brother and uncle had committed suicide in the last year and half and now Judith wanted to join them on the other side, thinking she would be with them again. The Victim Crisis Assistance and Referral Services (VCARS) team, of which I was a part of, had assisted the police at each of these suicides. There was no more we could do in that capacity because the team was not trained as counselors; although I was, I was not allowed to do anymore. I knew what to do for Judith on the spiritual level but I wondered if there was anything more I could do on a physical level.

My spiritual advisor, Tom Sawyer, (NOT the Huckleberry Finn one) told me I knew enough about the subject to write a poem that could prevent suicide.

Write a poem? I'm not a writer! Tom never said anything without reason and I knew if I didn't do as he suggested, and she succeeded in committing suicide, I would never forgive myself.

So, I sat down at my typewriter and asked, *Ok, what would LOVE write?* Three days later it was done. I didn't know if it would help. I only knew that reading it moved me to tears. I knew it had been inspired. I knew it was not only for those considering suicide ... it was for everyone! It was our story.

A 17-year-old friend was visiting and I asked him to read it to give me some feedback. I wanted to know if he would understand it and did he think it would help others.

Ten minutes later he asked, "How did you know?"

"How did I know what?" I asked.

"How did you know I was suicidal?" he replied.

Oh, my God! I didn't know! But LOVE obviously knew.

"I didn't understand all of it but one thing is clear," he continued, "I can't do it now."

Thank you, LOVE, for using me in this way. I wanted Tom to read it before I published it. We were both going to be in New York in two days so I waited to deliver it to him in person rather than mail it. That evening in meditation LOVE gave me the idea to make copies to bring to share with others, because it knew Tom would approve of it without any changes. I arrived with my copies and as I handed Tom one I got the idea to ask if I could read it to those assembled for the conference of a few hundred people.

The audience was wondering what the unplanned presentation was going to be as the master of ceremonies said a few words, announced my name and placed the microphone in front of me. I had had a lot of experience speaking in front of large audiences so I wasn't nervous; however, this experience was very unusual.

As soon as I began to speak my right arm began to shake, then it stopped. Then my left arm shook for a few moments and then stopped. I pressed the poem against the microphone stand to steady the booklet but that didn't help.

My right cheek began to shiver and shake like Jell-O, then the left cheek. My right thigh did its thing, then my left buttock was ready to take off ... *what the heck was happening?*

The tears were flowing down my face uncontrollably ... I tried to breathe. I looked at the audience and they too were crying. We were all being touched by LOVE, by our own story, by the truth!

The poem normally takes about seven minutes to read at the best of times. This evening it felt like it was taking forever. The master of ceremonies moved up to the microphone and said, "Seven point nine on the Richter scale and climbing," trying to lighten things up. A few chuckles were heard over the sniffing.

Eventually I finished the poem and the audience exploded to its feet and gave me what seemed like a five-minute standing ovation ... so many of us just couldn't stop crying.

Needless to say, my poem, LOVE's poem, was a winner. I sold every copy I brought and many more since to teachers, counselors, ministers and individuals. It is quite lengthy but well worth reading for everyone, not only those dealing with suicide. It is our story.

I know souls who have committed suicide and are truly lost on the other side. I know there are many still in their bodies contemplating suicide; so, every now and then LOVE moves me to mentally ask their spirits to all gather around, to listen while I read the poem out loud.

After it is over I pause and allow LOVE to inspire my words to help them do what is best.

I mentally talk to the spirits of those who have gathered. For those who were successful and now are on the other side, I also add some information that is not in the poem. Information that can release them from their 'hell' and send them HOME.

That release also affects their loved ones left behind. I sometimes get phone calls from one who has lost a loved one to suicide shortly after I have done this, reporting, "I dreamed of my brother last night. I now KNOW he is OK and I can let the guilt and pain go. I feel so much peace and LOVE."

I don't question whether this mental/spiritual communication is working or not, I know it is.

I don't know if Judith ever received the copy I sent her, I would hope so. If it hadn't been for her, this poem would never have been created, and I feel so humble to have been used to write it.

The following are just little bits of it ...

"My child, breathe deeply,
close your eyes and listen.
You are LOVE. You are LIGHT.

You are JOY. We are ONE.
Forget the illusion; remember reality.
You're still My Expression, My Being. My Sun.

...

Inside Your Body is a wonderful miracle,
The memory of Your Sacred I AM.
Inside each Cell is Divine identity,
The Truth about My great Hologram.

A hologram is really terrific.
To see the whole picture in 3D is fun.
Let us take out just a piece of the picture;
Reprint it, look at it, see it's still one!

I AM A Hologram. I AM The Big Picture.
I AM LOVE. I AM LIGHT. I AM TRUTH. I AM ONE.
You, My Child, are a piece of My Picture.
You are LOVE. You are LIGHT. You are TRUTH.
We are ONE.

That's what's amazing in a holographic picture,
Each little piece clearly shows the whole.
You, My Child, are a piece of My picture.
Look closely; you'll see a story untold!

Don't You get it? That is the miracle!
Inside of You is all that I AM!
You've looked outside You to get all Your answers.
All the while in You was The Big Bang!

...

Do You feel My LOVE? Do You see things clearer?
Do You see why suicide's a deadly affair?
Just look deep, look deep inside You.
That's where I AM; I've always been there!

Being touched by this LOVE
can make You Homesick.
That is your Light-showing you You.
There is a way to heal the pain real quick,
Just remember, I AM the LIGHT
And dear child so are You!

I AM the LIGHT. I AM in Your body.
I AM the LIGHT and that is the Truth!

And ends with ...

Your Body is My vehicle
Transporting Me to Earth.
All the gold and all the treasures
Cannot match what It is worth!

Some of the most rewarding work I have done has focused on suicide. One family called for help three days before Christmas. Their thirty-year-old son had committed suicide and was buried that day.

The information I shared enabled them to contact him, get some understanding of his actions, and to have a surprisingly enjoyable Christmas gathering a few days later.

The son's death had several positive outcomes; one was a gathering of ten to fifteen family members attending a four-hour workshop I conducted on a different subject each month.

When LOVE shines its light, even the darkest and deepest pit of pain experiences healing and peace. We need only ask.

LOVE ASKS ...

1. Have you ever been suicidal?

2. What stopped you?

3. Do you understand how you are a hologram of God?

A disciple:
I am worried about human suffering
all over the world.
What is the solution?

Spiritual leader:
The solution to our miseries lie within
central atom of our being, 'I'.

Once this central atom transcends to 'WE',
human sufferings can be resolved.

~ Santosh Kalwar ~
http://www.kalwar.com.np/

LOVE WORKS!
~ Play Ball ~

"It worked! I did as you suggested and it worked!" announced Gail at the restaurant. Gail had called me with good news and wanted to celebrate by taking me out to lunch.

"What worked?" I asked.

"That LOVE thing you told me to try," she replied. "Remember a few months ago, you suggested I ask what LOVE would do to find a job. I decided to give it a try and I got the idea to send a resume to a company I have always wanted to work for.

"I had my resume and cover letter done but couldn't seem to either put it in the mail or deliver it in person. I held onto that cursed resume for over two weeks! I knew I was qualified but for some reason I just couldn't get the darn thing off.

"I figured something must be holding me back for a reason. I then thought, 'Maybe I should change something.' I asked, "What would LOVE write?" and my eyes kept going to the part where you can add your hobbies. I had left it blank. No one would care if I played softball.

"But, after I asked the question it felt like I should include it and added that I had received the Most Valuable Player award three times.

"Suddenly everything felt Ok and I delivered it immediately. Guess what!

The new owner called and asked me to come in! I was excited but panicky. The owner himself called! It didn't take me long to find out why.

"The former owner sold his company because of ill health and hadn't been able to motivate his personnel the way he wanted to in the end. He handed the company over to this young man, he knew would find a way to give the company the boost it needed.

"He told me my softball background jumped out at him and turned his light on! He got so excited he challenged the company's competitor to a ball game before he even called me!"

"He must have been pretty sure you were still available," I commented.

"Maybe he talks to LOVE too," Gail giggled. "He told me, 'With you we can't lose!' He was so sure his new company could pull it off!"

"Did you feel pressured, Gail?" I asked.

"Not at all. I agreed with him. The rest of the team was really good; they just didn't have a pitcher. That's where I came in.

"I actually believe we would have ended up winners even if the other team had won because we had so much fun and melded so well as a team, it didn't really matter if we won or not.

Our spirits were so high! What a team! What a boss! What a company! I've only been there two months and it feels like I have come home.

"What's really nice was the way the boss made it clear my sports wasn't the only reason I was chosen. He compared my resume to the others on the short list and I was just as qualified if not more.

My ball experience was the icing on the cake.

"Isn't this the best! Ain't LOVE grand! Things have finally slowed down enough for me to be able to take you out to lunch to say thank you and to say, it works. LOVE really works!"

It sure does. LOVE knew if Gail had submitted her resume as soon as it was completed, her ball history would not have been included and she could have been bypassed, even with her glowing qualifications. Many people are bypassed for a variety of reasons.

LOVE knows where LOVE needs to be and LOVE wanted her on this company's team for more reasons than one. Her sports skills were needed to get her in the door.

What do you think she will say when asked how she got the job?

Who knows what LOVE will move her to say?

LOVE can be used for anything and everything.

LOVE loves to be everywhere serving everyone.

LOVE ASKS …

1. Do you truly know why you were hired?

2. Do you and your superiors/boss have the same intentions?

3. Do you feel you are in the right job, appreciated by your boss?

LOVE GAVE ME A BREAK
~ I Did It My Way ~

"Join us for the weekend at the cottage. We'll sit around the campfire, tell stories, roast marshmallows, sing songs, skinny-dip, and just do what we want, when we want, if we want," pleaded my friend Joan.

A weekend of rest and relaxation would be heavenly, I sighed. I had not had a day off in over three years. John kept saying, "You're living with me, not the girls. I need your help around here. Stay home."

I didn't want to stay home. I was tired of cleaning dog doo-doo, weeding, vacuuming, cooking, mowing lawns, and the rest that goes with one acre of land and hundreds of critters. John's attitude was making it quite easy for my human self to say, *I'm out of here. I deserve a day off. I don't care if John doesn't think I need a day off! I did!*

Here we go again, I thought. Part of me didn't want to ask, What would LOVE do? because it often asked me to do things I didn't want to do and I got the feeling this case would be no different ... however ... I really did want to do what LOVE wanted because I knew it would take care of my feelings and give me exactly what I needed.

To ensure I was not letting my human ego get the better of me I set up a code with LOVE.

If I see myself behind the wheel of my car, driving down the long driveway heading for the cottage that means yes/go; however, if I see myself cleaning dog kennels, weeding and working that means LOVE wants me to stay home/no go.

Hesitantly, I asked, *What would LOVE do?*

I suddenly saw myself behind the wheel of my car and got excited. *Yeah! Why do I keep going around in circles in my back yard and not down the driveway? Does that mean I stay home?*

I heard, "Yes."

Now I was really ticked off!

I gave LOVE an ultimatum, *You had better give me the desire to stay home, the joy, grace, kindness - whatever I need - and give it to me within the next two breaths because if I don't feel that desire to stay I am out of here!*

Within a flash I totally forgot my invitation for R & R. Shortly afterwards John entered the house and asked if I had made up my mind. "Yes. I've decided to stay home," I said joyfully. He was happier than a pig in poop, as they say on the farm. Guess how I spent my weekend? I kept driving around in circles in the backyard, delivering and picking up things for John in town. Something I LOVE to do.

Two of his kids called and asked if they could earn some extra money and ended up doing the inside and outside chores.

Every time I left the house I stopped at a flea market or yard sale. I bumped into friends I had not seen in ages and enjoyed lunch reliving old times.

I went to a movie and heard no complaints from John, who normally would have asked if we had won the lottery, because I was wasting money on movies. He thought that he had won, because I stayed home.

I was happy because I did all the things I love to do. I would not have had any R & R with my friends because they ended up having to deal with a mini flood at the cottage! At first it looked like LOVE was going to have me going in circles, which it did, perfectly, however, it wasn't to work. LOVE gave me the break I wanted, needed, and one that I truly enjoyed.

LOVE ASKS …

1. Do you believe you deserve some time off?

2. Are you ensuring you get it or are you afraid you'll get fired?

3. Are you letting someone else control your life, your joy?

The miracle is this:
the more we share the more we have.

~ Leonard Nimoy ~
http://www.imdb.com/name/nm0000559/bio

LOVE WALKS ON HOT COALS
~ Squishy Marshmallows ~

"I want to do that!" I told my husband excitedly.

"Do what?" he asked.

"Walk on fire!" I replied, pointing to the flyer I had received.

"Are you crazy? Why do you want to do that?"

"I don't know. I just want to."

A thousand dollars and a trip to California was a little more than my budget could handle in the early 1980s for a fire-walking course, so it would have to wait. Whenever I saw fire-walking ads in New Age magazines, the desire would surface but was never kindled. (Pun intended). A fire walk in the year 2000 would be a wonderful beginning for a new millennium. Finally, I was able to participate.

The fire maker, Pat McConnelly a Texan, led us through the preparations necessary to walk the coals without burning our feet.

"This is the largest and hottest fire I have ever created," he reported sensing our concern. "It is 1500 degrees!"

"Ouch! That could be dangerous," whispered a few. We chanted, sang, and danced around the fire and broke a one-inch thick piece of wood, eight by ten inches, with the heel of our hand to raise our vibrations, to put us in an altered state.

We did exercises to let go of painful memories and decided what we wanted to manifest after the fire walk.

When preparing to break the board, Pat instructed, "Feel the energy come up your spine and out your solar plexus. Look and aim past the board."

Two people held a board for those who chose the open-heel-of the-hand technique. Some chose to slice through the board towards the ground like a knife with the little finger edge of the hand.

"Step up when you feel ready," Pat instructed.

I felt ready. I could feel the energy coming up my spine and with my eyes closed I let that board have it! I punched out so hard and fast and slid off the side of the board towards the holder, I almost giving her a black eye.

"Oops! I'm sorry," I apologized sheepishly. "I had my eyes closed. I was doing it from within."

"You have to come out, Caroline. It's time. You have to be here to do this," the holder advised wisely, having done this many times herself.

Those words sent shivers of affirmation throughout my body. *Yes, it is time to claim my power, to be here! I am ready! I am here! My eyes are open.* I looked at the tree six feet beyond the board. The energy rose and exploded out of me through the board! I hit so hard and so fast one of the holders was spun around and fell down.

Everyone cheered and applauded. The holder shook herself off and got ready for the next person.

I did it! I did it! I thought. *I know how to do this!* That power was within me, bursting to come out!

"Now," continued Pat "when it came time for the fire walk, the energy you felt with the board, is what you must feel walking around the fire. When it is time to walk the fire, you will know it. When you stand at the head of the fire it will call out to you.

"You will feel an opening up of your solar plexus. You will feel peace and a pull to do the walk. If you think this is easy and you don't feel any tension to start with, you are the one who should not walk the fire," he cautioned.

"Like with the breaking of the wood, don't look at the fire, look past it and start walking. Don't stop till you have walked through it and have both feet on the grass."

I walked and walked around that twelve-foot-long pit feeling absolutely nothing. *Am I one who should not walk it?* I wondered. Several had already gone through.

I had been praying for this opportunity for almost twenty years and really wanted to do it ... but I didn't feel the same physical sensations previously felt when splitting the board.

Around and around the pit I went. I then thought, *Well what do I do when I need to make a decision?*

I asked, *What would LOVE do?*

I did just that and as I was coming to the head of the fire ... I felt, *it's time*. I felt peaceful. I stepped forward without doubt, even though it wasn't as Pat had instructed. It was like walking on marshmallows!

I felt no heat. No pain and was standing on the grass smiling like a kid in a candy store!

Yea! I did it! My mom, who was in her seventies, congratulated me and then did the same thing. We both did it!

I continued walking around the circle to keep the energy high for the others who had yet to walk. *I can repeatedly walk these coals without stopping ... step in, walk to the end, step out and walk around to the front walk again and again*, I kept thinking. *Is that my ego wanting to show off?* I continued walking around the pit; the thought to repeat the fire walk would not leave me.

Again I asked my question *What would LOVE do?* and as I came to the front, without thinking, I stepped in and walked through the fire. Again, it felt like marshmallows.

I stepped out and suddenly got bumped from behind by my friend Cecile.

"Thank you. Thank you. Thank you." Cecile cried. "I was asking God to send someone in front of me to lead the way just as you were rounding the corner and He sent you to me."

The urge to walk the coals was gone. I had done what I had come to do. The next morning as I was doing the dishes and reviewing my fire walk I wondered, *Why didn't I feel the sensation Pat cautioned us about? I had had it with the board-breaking exercise.*

"Don't you understand how LOVE works yet?" I heard in my mind. "I, LOVE, give you the desire to do something because I want you to do it for whatever reason.

"You had prayed for this for many years and you could have done it then if you had just said, "Send me what I need." I would have sent you the money.

"Finally, I had another chance to use you and I gave you everything you needed to do it.

"It would have been a waste of LOVE energy to give you the sensation Pat was talking about, just to take it away again. You have developed enough trust in Me to know you would be ok as you were. All you ever have to do is ask," came the explanation.

Whether it was just my imagination or LOVE actually talking to me didn't really matter anymore. All I knew is LOVE took care of me again … and again … and again. The desire to fire-walk was now gone. What an evening it had been! Twenty-five of us were successful.

A man in his seventies was not. He made a few mistakes …

1. He sat the whole time while we walked around the fire.
2. He did not join us in the energy raising exercises to prepare.
3. He simply got up and walked directly into the pit.
4. The last thing said before he stepped forward was, "There's no fool like an old fool." That was another mistake!
5. He took the first step, looked down and immediately flashed back to time when he and his buddies had been in a fire and he was the only one to survive.
6. He felt his foot burn and instead of stepping back, his pride … or guilt … moved him forward. That was another mistake!

He ended up with third degree burns on both of his feet. He spent many days in the hospital blaming no one but himself.

A fire-walk provides an opportunity to symbolically walk through fears, pains and limitations that no longer serve us so we can exit purified and ready to be our full selves. It is not something to try without proper preparation!

LOVE ASKS ...

1. Have you ever, would you ever, walk on hot coals?

2. What motivates you to do things? Desire? Guilt? Pride?

3. What frightens you and stops you from facing it?

*You may find the worst enemy
or best friend in yourself.*

~ English Proverb ~

LOVE CLEANS UP
~ Self Respect Gains More Respect ~

He was often complimented on how sharp he looked in his crisply ironed shirts and smart suits, but Mr. Clean he was not!

"I've tried everything to get him to simply drop his clothes into the hamper when he undresses," cried Debbie.

You could tell his wife was exhausted. She worked eight long stressful hours cleaning other people's houses, came home to prepare dinner, help the kids with their homework and then do her own work. Housework was the last thing on her mind.

James did not help. Wet towels were left on the floor in the shower. She tripped over his shoes and clothing. He really was a good provider and father but he was a slob!

"I even put an open wicker hamper in the bedroom next to his chair and one in the bathroom so he can just peel off his clothes and drop them into the basket! Where do they land? On the floor beside the hamper!

"He is a fantastic basketball player. I've seen him sink baskets from center court! He can throw a baseball through a little hole why can't he hit a great big hole with his stupid socks?" she moaned.

Her mother, mother in law, sisters and friends all made suggestion that produced no results. At least his suit coat was on the doorknob.

She hoped he might put it on the special suit rack on a butler's chair that she bought him for Christmas.

She was at her wits end that Thursday. She had worked overtime and came home unusually tired to find everyone as cranky as she was.

"I have a special meeting tomorrow, make sure my blue shirt is ironed," James ordered.

No please or thank you Ma'am! she thought. That was the last straw!

She collapsed onto her bed and cried. *What can I do? I am so-o-o-o tired! What would LOVE do?* popped into her mind.

"It was as if you were standing in the room saying those words once again, but this time I heard them," she told me the next day.

"Suddenly, I started to giggle and laughed out loud. I knew what to do!" she continued.

"I started kicking his shirt and socks and other stuff under the bed! I was shocked at my bravery!"

"It's your job to do my clothes and take care of me," James had told her more than once. *What will he say?* she wondered, but didn't care for the first time in their ten-year marriage.

The next day he got dressed and went to work wearing his good blue shirt that Debbie had already ironed last laundry day.

The next night she did the same thing. She kicked his clothes under the bed wondering how long it would be before he would notice his supply of clean clothes was dwindling.

Four days later James asked, "Did you do any ironing? I can't find any clean shirts."

"If they were in the hamper, they got washed and ironed," Debbie replied. "I don't remember doing any." She was surprised the giggles inside her belly hadn't turned into fear at the possibility of getting him angry.

"I can't find any," James yelled from the dressing room. Debbie remained silent as James continued his search.

"Where do you remember seeing them last?" Debbie asked, coaching him. She felt like saying, "You're getting warmer" as he got close to the bed.

"You're getting colder" as he moved away. She knew not to push her luck, but what amazed her was the inner peace she was feeling!

He finally bent down and looked under the bed.

The cursing, yelling and name calling that followed would have been funny if it hadn't been so sad. She knew he would regret his words later. Still, she felt only peace.

He was getting later and later for work. He took out the iron and ironing board and ironed his own dirty shirt. There were no good-bye kisses that day. She was greeted by a cold shoulder when she got home.

Debbie never said a word and neither did James. It was never mentioned again. His actions spoke louder than words. He began joyfully slam dunking his dirty clothes into the hampers from that moment on, truly becoming the squeaky Mr. Clean everyone thought he was, and began thanking Debbie for taking such good care of him and the kids.

Debbie also changed. The more she honored, respected and valued herself, the more others did. It's amazing the things LOVE suggests to solve our problems. It knows everything about everyone involved and is ready to guide us if we would only ask for what we need to clean up our act.

LOVE ASKS ...

1. Do you get the respect you think you deserve?

2. If not, why not?

3. Did Debbie's story inspire you to trust LOVE a tad more?

LOVE IS PSYCHIC
~ The Perfect Recipe ~

"This is going to be such fun," I shared with my husband as I was preparing for the evening. I was looking forward to going to the live theatre with my friends and the celebration afterwards at our home. I wanted to offer my guests some drinks and dessert and wondered what to prepare.

What would LOVE make? I wondered. *Ah, this new recipe looks yummy. I can prepare it ahead of time and leave it in the refrigerator. Oh, it's also sugar free. Great for my diet.*

What a night it was! Our friend Jessie, had the lead role in Jesus Christ Superstar and was amazing! I hadn't realized how magnificent his voice was till then, powerful yet gentle, joyful yet full of angst. He really made me feel the part he was playing. The standing ovation was well deserved by the whole cast and when all the congratulations were over we proceeded to our home for a more intimate celebration.

I offered my guests the new dessert and 'Judas,' I couldn't remember his true name, refused saying, "No, I'm sorry. I don't eat desserts."

'Why not?" I asked innocently.

"I'm diabetic," he replied.

"Well what a coincidence! This dessert is sugar free! You can enjoy it!"

"You must be psychic," he laughed while accepting the dessert

"Aren't we all?" I challenged, realizing, LOVE is the best psychic in the house.

LOVE knew exactly what would help my diet and also took care of my guest's special need.

LOVE definitely was the 'superstar' that night.

LOVE ASKS ...

1. Are you more willing to ask LOVE what to prepare for meals for your family, friends, yourself?

2. Can you trust it KNOWS what is best for all?

3. What else can you begin to trust LOVE with?

LOVE DELIVERS MY CAR
~ Patience Is A Virtue ~

The insurance company wrote off my deluxe van after my accident in the States in January 1994. I was newly divorced in December '93 and didn't have a 'real' job providing a steady income. The life of a psychic/healer is not usually a profitable one when one accepts LOVE offerings as payment. The bus stopped in front of my apartment so what did I need a car for?

In 1995 my life changed. I met a wonderful man, moved to the country and was still unconcerned about having a car; after all, John had a truck. Most women lose themselves totally in serving their new love, until it is time to reclaim their lives. I was no different.

The thought of having my own car only entered my mind when John had the truck and my need to be more independent returned. I had been able to come and go as I pleased most of my life. I was also feeling the need to begin traveling again to do my work.

One day, when I was stuck at home suffering from cabin fever, I decided to use my tools to manifest a car. My best manifestation tool was the Magical Question ... What would LOVE do?

"Pause. A car is on its way to you. You will win one or be given one," was the answer. It was the same answer every time I asked the question.

I entered the occasional contest for a car but never won.

"Pause. It's on its way to you." I would hear every time I bought a ticket.

It was as though LOVE was chuckling at my impatience, hinting I was wasting my money buying tickets. It was like I was not going to be required to spend a penny to get my car, not even buy a ticket. Guess if I was going to win it someone would have to buy me the winning ticket. LOVE knew why … it was on its way to me!

On my fiftieth birthday my sweetheart gave me the most beautiful gold Buick Regal!

What else would you buy a queen other than a Regal! And gold was the perfect color for someone attracting more abundance in her life.

John often said I cheated because it came from him. I really didn't care who LOVE used to deliver it. It sent me my car! Thank you. Thank you. Thank you, LOVE and John. I paused … and it did come to me.

LOVE ASKS …

1. Have you ever wanted something and KNEW you were going to get it?

2. What would YOU like to have LOVE bring you?

3. Do you have the patience to wait or will you give up and say it doesn't work?

LOVE FINDS MY BIRTH MOTHER
~ A Wish Come True ~

"Do you know what Dana had the nerve to say?" I yelled at Mom as I burst into the house, crying.

"What?" Mom asked, quite surprised by my sudden entry.

"She said the reason you make me do all the work is because I am adopted!" I cried.

"Why are you getting so upset?" she asked as I continued to cry.

Being adopted was not a good thing in our neighborhood in the '50s. You were someone else's reject, the target of people's jokes. No one was considered 'chosen' in those days.

When she saw how upset I was she took me into her bedroom, showed me the papers and admitted the truth. *I WAS adopted!* I could have died!

"We adopted you because we were told we couldn't have any children and then we got six more on our own. You could say you were a good luck charm", Mom added trying to cheer me up.

"We never treated you any differently than the rest. We actually forgot you weren't originally ours."

That explained why I had red hair and everyone else was blonde. That explained why I always felt so different, like I didn't belong. I was the quietest eleven-year-old from that moment on.

I simply stopped talking. I would cry the moment anybody asked about or admired my red hair. I hated it!

I couldn't blame my parents for my pulling away. If anyone got the best of things it was usually me. Relatives often felt sorry for me because I was adopted and gave me more attention than my brothers and sisters.

As a teen, I began writing, Dear someone ... I would write twenty to thirty pages every night when I was supposed to be doing my homework. It's a wonder I ever passed any classes in school.

Whenever I did speak it was to ask, *Why?* I questioned everything and everyone. I wanted to know everything from every angle possible, especially God. I never did finish high school. I began to play hooky. I felt completely inadequate in everything even though I received awards for almost everything I did.

I decided to run away and join the military. I excelled for sixteen years in the Canadian Air Force and decided to leave it to begin my spiritual journey (although I did not word it that way at the time).

My husband and I often took in young people, one of the teens passed as my daughter because she had red hair. She came to us because of her troubled background. She had recently given her newborn up for adoption and kept asking if she had done the right thing.

Her questioning caused my bottled-up feelings to surface, so we decided to join a group for adoptees, adoptive parents, and birth parents who wanted to support each other. The pain I saw on the birth mothers' faces caused my heart to break.

If I can do only one thing, I want to tell my birth mother I turned out ok. (Some might argue that point). I want to tell her my parents gave me a good life and that she made the right decision to give me up. I want to say thank you.

In our group, every single birth mother wondered every single day if she had done the right thing. I wanted to end my birth mother's possible pain and guilt. There are many reunion stories that turn out to be horror stories but I didn't anticipate that when I decided to find my birth mother.

Some of my siblings couldn't understand why I needed to search and felt I was rejecting them. I tried to explain the pain I was trying to relieve.

Am I causing the only family I know pain by trying to relieve the pain of someone I don't know? What would LOVE do?

"Go. Search," came the reply.

While I was visiting my parents for an entirely different reason, Mom began acting like a private investigator, asking relatives and friends all kinds of questions. Some actually believed I was my dad's sister's child. Nope.

When I say 'Mom and Dad' I mean the parents who brought me up since I was ten days old.

As a Reiki Master, I had learned how to go into the future to manifest things, so I began using that knowledge to get things moving. I made my own inquiries.

I went to the Children's Aid Society that had arranged the adoption and was given general information like: my birth mother was the eldest of seven ... so was I! She Loved sports ...I was a Physical Education Instructor! My father was in the Air Force ... so was I! He was married to someone else at the time I was conceived. My birth mother's name told me she was French Catholic - so was I!

I was born in another city when my birth mother was twenty-seven, which was pretty old to be unmarried and have a child out of wedlock in 1947.

Ten days later, I was in my new home with the family I was destined to grow up with. One of my brothers knew someone who could help me. Fifteen minutes later he called and gave me my birth mother's cousin's name and address.

I called the Children's Aid Society to ask if I was on the right path.

"If I were you I would call her up and ask her to register with the adoption disclosure agency," came the worker's reply. That was a Yes!

Shortly afterward, Mom was talking to my birth mother on the phone under the guise of doing some research.

"I am doing a family tree and notice we have the same last name," my adoptive Mom began.

"Give me the phone," I said. That was a lie and I didn't want to put either mother through that.

"Hello Mrs. _____, my name is Caroline McIntosh. I was born on June 23, 1947 in _____to a woman who has the same family name as you.

"Would you please do me a favor?" I continued, "If you come across a woman in your family who reveals that she has given up a child for adoption would you discreetly tell her I turned out alright. I had a good life and family. Tell her she made the right decision and say thank you to her for me."

My birth mother very tensely replied, "I don't know anyone who did that," wanting to end the conversation.

"Well, if you come across a woman who has, please pass on the message, she did the right thing and thank you."

Again she denied knowing anyone who had done that, so I gently repeated the message, gave my thanks, and said farewell. I did not want to cause her any more stress. It was done. I got exactly what I wanted.

Most people would question why I did not pursue it. It never entered my mind to do so because I had done exactly what I had set out to do. It wasn't until I got to my home in Kingston that I realized, *Dang! I don't know what I look like!*

Now I was as upset as the others in my adoption group because I hadn't pursued it more.

The leader of the adoption group was a woman who, at sixteen, was forced to give up her newborn.

Her sixteen-year-old boyfriend was forced out of town with the threat of going to jail.

She was now in her forties, married and searching for her son. She began the group because she wanted to talk to others in the same predicament and to possibly get help in finding him.

Because she often acted as a mediator in reunions I asked her to contact my birth mother to arrange a meeting for us. She made the call. My birth mother was very upset and denied everything until she heard my friend's story.

It is common for birth mothers to fear the child will cause trouble if there is not a meeting of some sort. For that reason only, she agreed to talk to me. I was told to call her at exactly 2 p.m. on the next Sunday afternoon.

I must admit, I was nervous as I dialed her number and then the cosmic giggles in my belly began ...*Oh My God! LOVE has such a wonderful sense of humor ... it's Mother's Day!*

She answered the phone. I assured her I only wanted to meet her and would cause no trouble. She agreed to a meeting the following Tuesday after her doctor's appointment. She would have a reason to be in town. That would give me Monday to travel. Once again I used my Reiki Master's knowledge to go into the future to make things as easy as possible, especially for her.

I arrived at the meeting place half an hour early. I wanted to watch her come in.

She looks like me, I thought as a woman came my way. We made eye contact.

"Are you Mrs._____?" I asked. A look of panic crossed her face,

"No!" she replied as she ran out the door. *Oh! Have I frightened her away?* No …I realized it wasn't her.

I waited some more. It was still early.

Another woman entered and moved in my direction. She looked more like me than the last one but she was a 'bag lady', a street person, looking very disheveled and worn out.

Wow! Am I ready for anything? I wondered. *No, it couldn't be her,* logic told me. The last time I was in town I drove past her perfect little house with its perfectly manicured yard. She wasn't a 'bag lady.'

I waited some more. A tall, very slim, very dark-haired woman entered the store.

If she hadn't looked like she was looking for someone, I would not have noticed her. She looked nothing like me!

"Are you Mrs. _____?" I asked.

She nodded.

"I am Caroline McIntosh." She looked puzzled.

"Oh, my maiden name was Lafleur," I added.

"You called me Sandra Ann _____. Is there some place we could sit and talk, maybe have a cup of coffee?" I asked.

"Across the street, there's a Chinese restaurant. We can go there, but I don't have much time. I have to catch my bus," she replied nervously as she led the way out the door.

I couldn't get over how different we looked and how calm and peaceful I felt. Most reunions are teary–

eyed, but not this one. I found out she did marry, had three children and her husband was still alive.

I also found out she was like me on the inside when I was younger; ulcers, migraine headaches, a worrier, lacking self-esteem.

We visited for about half an hour. I questioned her about my father but she said she couldn't remember who he was. I felt she didn't want me to look for him. She seemed very worried that someone would discover her secret shame.

It was time to take the bus. Both of us were going in the same direction so we traveled together.

I sensed there were others on the bus who knew her so when she got off I did not offer her a hug because it would have been very difficult for her to explain why she would be hugging a stranger.

She asked me to call her when I was back in town. I was invited to visit as a friend but I knew it would have been too difficult for her.

I often returned to town to do TV interviews and one time Mom was on the show with me.

When I called my birth mom after the show, the first thing out of her mouth was, "Oh your mother is so beautiful!"

My birth mother does not feel she is a pretty woman and probably gave sex to get LOVE (as many women have) and voila, got me! I now knew why I didn't like my looks when I was young. The mother's thoughts become the child's when a fetus.

I called her about four times since then and each time I was concerned someone else would answer the phone, so I stopped calling.

That was until I moved back to town in 1993.

Imagine, I moved into an apartment six streets away from her. I called her up and invited her to drop in for a visit when she was out for her walk. She replied that would be nice but never did. A year later I moved.

She entered my mind so many times it began to bother me.

What if she's dying and wants to say something. What if she wants to get in touch with me and she doesn't know where I am. I'm not even listed in the phone book! What would LOVE do?

I mailed her a copy of my first children's book, THE FIREFLY FLIGHTBOOK, with a cover letter asking her to read it so I, the author, could call her up later to get some feedback from her as I had done with several other people.

I did follow up. She thanked me for the book but said she couldn't read it because her sight was going. She would get her daughter to read it to her grandchildren. I sensed she was not alone so our call was very short.

Every now and then I wondered how she was doing.

She would now be in her eighties. LOVE told me to call her again before it's too late. I know it will move me to do so when the time is right.

FOLLOW UP: In 2010 I was house-sitting a few streets from where I knew my birth mother lived.

I called her home and left a message. Her daughter, my half-sister, returned my call. She proceeded to tell me her mother had died in 1995 and then asked how I knew her mother and why was I calling.

Ummm... What would LOVE say?

"Tell her the truth," was the reply. Needless to say, she didn't believe me.

I replied with, "I wouldn't believe it either. I would want proof."

She asked me to describe her and when I did, she was silent. I knew how difficult it was for her and didn't want to cause any trouble.

I concluded the call with, "If you want to know any more about me, do not hesitate to call. I would be glad to meet with you."

I've often been asked if I knew my birth parents and end my story with, "My mom was tall, flat chested with very dark hair. I guess my dad (who I haven't met) is the one who's short, with red hair and big boobs" lol. I used to be built like Dolly Parton, the big busted country singer / actress/songwriter.

As I write this I know, I know I need to contact her so she can connect with her mother using LOVE'S MAGICAL CONNECTION. It is time ...

LOVE ASKS ...

1. What would YOU have said in my place when asked why I was calling my birth mother?

2. How do you feel about adopted children?

3. How would you feel if YOU were adopted?

It is in your hands to make life miserable or happy.
No religion, spiritual leaders or knowledge will ever make you fully satisfied."

~ Santosh Kalwar ~
http://www.kalwar.com.np/

LOVE HUMBLES A TEACHER
~ She Learns Something New ~

It was Sunday afternoon and I was beginning to look forward to going home to soak my weary feet after the three-day Women's Fair. People of all ages stopped at my booth and asked about my work and me. As impossible as some friends may think it is, I was almost talked–out and was looking forward to the bliss of silence.

The kids provided the most fun for me and entertainment for the passersby as I measured their auras and did muscle testing. I guess LOVE wanted to save the best for last.

Two women stopped at my table and began reading my material.

"We are teachers," one lady said. "What exactly do you do with the children that is different from what is already being taught in schools?"

"I help them with anger management," I began.

"We do that!" she interrupted.

"I give them tools to develop self-esteem," I continued.

"We do that too!" she added quite aggressively.

"I use techniques and tools that are quite different from what is presently used," I said beginning to wonder why LOVE sent me this challenge so late in the weekend.

As she went on and on about what they did I went within and asked my usual question, *What would LOVE say to this woman?*

Immediately I chuckled and thought, *Lady I am about to knock your socks off!* I don't recall ever saying or thinking such words in the past with anyone but they felt quite appropriate at this moment. She was in for a surprise! LOVE knew she had to experience what I was talking about for herself.

"Would you be willing to try a little experiment?" I asked.

"I bet you can't hold your arm out at shoulder height and keep it there if I apply a little pressure on your wrist while your friend is thinking a negative thought about herself." I challenged.

"I don't believe you! Try it," she replied wanting to prove me wrong. She raised her arm and locked her shoulder. I put two fingers on her locked wrist and lightly tried to press her arm down and it wouldn't budge.

"Now," I said to the other teacher, "think a negative thought about yourself. It makes no difference what it is and don't tell us what it is."

"And you try to keep your arm up while I apply a little pressure," I said to the one with her arm up. Her arm quickly lowered with little pressure applied by only one finger.

"Come on!" I said, "Be tough! Be strong!" prompting her to try again and again.

Her arm came down every time! I then asked her friend to think a positive thought. This time when I tried to push the woman's arm downward it wouldn't budge. I began using my whole hand and applied more pressure ... still her arm stayed up. She was in shock. Her eyes almost popped out of her head.

"See," I continued, "thoughts, energy put out by others, affect everyone, whether they know it or not, unless they know how to recognize it and protect themselves.

"There is a force within us all that connects us, unites us, picks up things from others and registers them in our bodies. That force is LOVE. Is it no wonder a mother knows when her child is in trouble!"

I then offered to measure her energy field, her aura, with the copper energy rods I held in my hands.

After she gave me the ok, I placed the parallel rods about two inches in front of her and began backing up. I had moved about three yards when the rods separated.

"This is how big your energy field is at this moment," I said, adding, "actually, it's probably larger than that but these instruments are very crude."

I then asked her to close her eyes and think of something that caused her stress. When the rods became parallel I began walking towards her.

At approximately six inches away from her body the rods crossed.

"Open your eyes," I instructed. "Look at how small your energy field is now," I said.

"All the flu bugs, viruses, negative energy and so forth, are right under your nose. Do you think it will be easier to catch them now?"

She looked a little pale.

"Close your eyes again. Think about something or someone you LOVE!" I continued.

The rods became parallel and I backed up once more. I ended up at least 15 yards away from her before the rods separated.

"Open your eyes," I shouted over the crowd that had gathered.

"Look at how big you are now!" I said, delighted.

"Where is all that negative stuff now?"

"I can't believe it! I can't believe it!" she repeated over and over and over again.

"These are just two things that I do with the kids to show them how their thoughts and feelings make an impression on others.

"I give them the tools necessary to know if the negativity they are experiencing is theirs or someone else's. I then show them how to take care of themselves and their loved ones."

"Do you do this in schools?" she asked excitedly.

I smiled and I decided not to answer right away. I knew she would remember that that was why we began this conversation in the first place.

"Would you come to our school?" she asked sheepishly when she realized what she had asked.

"Gladly," I replied. "Let's set a date now."

LOVE knew how to put the icing on my cake that weekend. I didn't sell enough books and CD's to pay for my booth, (I probably talked too much) but I sure made a lot of contacts, changed the way some people looked at themselves and others and left a lasting impression on one particular teacher.

LOVE ASKS ...

1. Do you know how big your energy field/aura is?

2. Do you know if the anger you are feeling belongs to you?

3. Are your thoughts and feeling make others weaker or stronger?

Love is the Krazy Glue of the Universe
and it feels so-o-o-o good!
That's why I'm stuck on you!

~ I Am Caroline ~
www.IAmCaroline.com

LOVE SAYS I'M OK
~ There Are No Mistakes ~

It was her second visit to the Women's Center that month. The information shared two weeks earlier had obviously made a difference. She walked in taller, made more eye contact, smiled and said, "Hi Caroline."

"Hi Jane." I smiled back thrilled that she had returned.

A month prior, I had been at a presentation given by Legal Aid for the Women's Center clients and listened to the horror stories the women shared about the abuse they had experienced not only from their husbands and family but also from the police and the legal system.

Legal Aid was there to let them know what their rights were and to provide counseling throughout the whole courtroom procedure. I was new to the community and didn't want to ruffle any feathers however I knew something was missing. I asked a simple question and got a simple answer.

"Do the women get any emotional or spiritual counseling during this procedure to help them deal with what is happening?"

"No. Next question?" and the speaker moved on.

That's what was missing. I knew something had to be done, but what? *What would LOVE do?*

I should have seen it coming by now, "Offer your services one day a week", came the reply.

I guess I could squeeze in one day at the Center. The news spread quickly.

Every hour from 9 a.m. until 5 p.m. on Wednesdays I listened to women cry their hearts out, begging for relief and some peace.

It was Jane's second visit.

She had spent time in prison for killing her partner, aborted two fetuses, had prostituted herself to support her drug and alcohol addiction and was trying to clean up her act. Society had rejected her totally.

I sensed something special was about to happen. I had provided her with an exercise that would allow her to recognize LOVE in ways she'd never thought of before and she was back for more, ready to see and love herself in a new way, and I was thrilled to be a part of it.

I thought I was going to share the Natural Process™ with her but when I double-checked with what would LOVE do? I was moved to tell her the student /teacher story.

I wrote SA - Sally and SB - Mary at the bottom of my writing pad and began, "Here are Sally and Mary destined to become Teacher A and Teacher B (as I wrote TA and TB at the top of the page).

"They are so alike they could be twins - same neighborhood, size, age, beliefs everything ... both keen and eager to do their best."

With my pen I begin to draw a line slowly connecting Sally on the bottom of the page to TA at the top of the page while saying, "Sally knows the rules of the road, school, church, family, community; she is the ideal student, volunteers, excels, grows up, is a

model of perfection, gets all kinds of awards, knows how to walk the straight and narrow so well she becomes Teacher A in life in record time. Ta Da!"

Now I move to Mary and start moving my pen to connect it to TB at the top of the page but this story is a quite different.

"Mary began her journey exactly the same as Jane - with the same dedication, discipline, knowing the rules. But curiosity led her on a few detours. Drugs, booze, relationship problems, trouble with everyone, ends up in prison, gets out, and on and on and finally becomes Teacher B after much searching and healing."

I drew a very twisted, curving line from bottom to the top.

"What a twisted life this one has had," I say, acting pooped, exhausted from all the hard work.

"Yeah, I know," Jane added, "That's like my story."

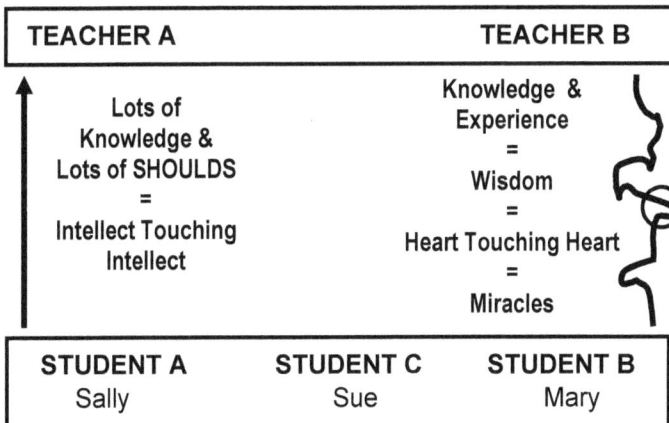

TEACHER A		TEACHER B
Lots of Knowledge & Lots of SHOULDS = Intellect Touching Intellect		Knowledge & Experience = Wisdom = Heart Touching Heart = Miracles
STUDENT A Sally	**STUDENT C** Sue	**STUDENT B** Mary

I continued, "Along comes Student C – Sue and all three are at the coffee shop socializing. Sue asks a question.

I then look at Jane and ask her, "Who do you think is best qualified to answer that question, Teacher A - Sally or Teacher B – Mary?

"That depends on the question," Jane replied, "but more than likely it is Mary because s/he has been through so much, has experienced more."

"Good answer," I replied. "Many would agree with you." I knew I had to push her buttons and knew exactly how to do it, so I continued.

"Some actually say it would be the one who was most disciplined, dedicated, obeyed the rules and was no problem to society, like Teacher A – Sally."

Jane frowned as I continued, "Let's imagine the conversation that could take place, Jane. Sally would probably say, 'Well you should do this. You should do that. You should read this book. So and so said this,' etc.'

"There are a lot of shoulds in Sally's vocabulary. Lots of knowing, book knowing, someone else's knowing. She has a lot of knowledge but it's all in the head and when she speaks it will be intellect touching intellect and not much change will take place.

"On the other hand, Teacher B - Mary might not say much. She might flash back to one of the little detours on her journey through the drug problems and say something that may have nothing to do with

Sue's original question but, touches her in such a way that it moves her to tears asking, "Are you psychic? How did you know? How did you know I had a drug problem?"

"Mary has knowledge plus experience, which equals wisdom and that always comes from the heart, especially one that has healed.

"Mary will be inspired to ask Sue a question that has nothing to do with the original question, however, it is perfect. It zoomed in on the exact problem the student had.

"Sue will be astounded, 'How did you know what my real problem was?" she'll ask.

Words, feelings, anything that leaves a heart will always touch another heart and that's when miracles happen. Speakers become mesmerizing, hypnotic, charismatic, even intoxicating.

"I am not saying Sally is not a good teacher. LOVE knows exactly who to send to whom for help. If someone is still in his or her head and not ready to have his or her heart opened, Sally would be perfect with her shoulds and should nots.

"When I used to airbrush t-shirts my best seller was, "Don't should on me and I won't should on you." I added.

We both laughed at that because when you say it quickly it doesn't sound like it is written. I went on because I knew she was fully absorbing what I was sharing.

"So you mean to tell me I had the right answer," she questioned. "That I was ok?"

"Ok?" I replied excited, "Not only are you ok, you are SO loved!"

"I am loved?" she whispered shyly.

"Yes" I continued. "I am so in awe of a soul that has so much love it volunteers to go through a very difficult journey just to gather the information and experience necessary to ask that one question!"

I paused and let that sink in.

"Can you imagine a LOVE that grand? A journey much like your own, Jane. You, Jane, can so easily touch people than I cannot because of what you have been through.

"Besides, like I told you last time we spoke, each and every one of us is absolute perfection in the Creator's eyes. Each of us is an atom in the body of God and God loves every part of Itself equally. No one is ever loved more or less by the Creator, by LOVE."

"You mean to tell me I am good? I'm Ok?" she whispered with tears slowly sliding down her cheeks.

"Good?" I whispered. "Not only are you good and ok, you are SO loved!"

"You mean I am good and I am loved?" Her eyes got bigger, the tears flowed quicker and she began to shake and catch her breath.

It was almost too good to be true. She cried and cried and I joined in feeling so blessed to have witnessed LOVE in action.

We cried tears of joy and release until we couldn't cry anymore; then Jane raised her head, blew her nose, looked at me, and then we started laughing. We laughed until our sides and cheeks hurt.

I was thrilled because laughter is a sign that her right brain had kicked in and a healing was taking place. I could see her mind shifting and absorbing the significance of what had just happened.

She wasn't bad anymore! She was loved!

She could use her past to be of service to others who had had similar experiences. She now considered herself one of LOVE's helpers and realized she could make a difference, and that she mattered.

She realized that nothing had been a mistake. It has all been on the job training to qualify her to do her soul's work.

That was the last time I saw Jane. The word on the street was that she had registered for further education and was volunteering at a drug addiction center, cleaning and cooking and realizing her dream of helping others was possible.

She was not only gathering knowledge by going back to school, her experiences provided her with the wisdom necessary to be LOVE's servant to other lost souls, who had had similar life experiences, finding their way back to peace and self-love.

She could be of service to them, help them greatly without even saying, "I've been there." The minute she starts to speak, it will be heart touching heart and that's when miracles happen.

LOVE ASKS ...

1. Do you have knowledge or wisdom?

2. Can you see how a negative experience you've had now qualifies you to be of service to others?

3. How often do you 'should' people?

THE CHILDREN

Look into their eyes.
Do you see Me?

Listen to them.
Do you hear Me?

They have something very important
To share with you
On My Behalf!

THEY ARE YOUR TEACHERS!

*Love yourself first
and everything else falls into line.
You really have to love yourself
to get anything done in this world.*

~ Lucille Ball~
http://www.imdb.com/name/nm0000840/bio

LOVE'S MAGICAL CONNECTION
~ The Tie That Binds ~

Six-year-old Nicky's parents were divorced. He lived with his mother and hadn't spoken to his father in at least four months. Because he was so afraid he would never see his dad again he often said ugly, nasty things to his mother. He yelled, screamed and cursed, blaming her for everything.

He wouldn't stop until she began hitting him in the face and on the head. He began thinking; *Every time I speak I get hit*; so, he stopped speaking.

Nicky hadn't spoken a word in three months and no one knew why. He wouldn't tell anyone … no matter who asked him. He moved his head up and down saying "Uh huh" for "Yes" and left and right saying "Un huh" for "No."

He was getting in trouble at school and with the police. The only place he felt safe was with his grandmother, but he wouldn't tell her how bad things were at home. She took him to the doctor to find out what was wrong.

"He is severely tongue-tied," Dr. Joe explained "He may never speak again unless you find out why."

Nicky's grandmother knew I worked with children so she asked for my help.

When he entered my apartment the thought, *Nicky needs something to help him feel connected to his father* popped into my mind. *What should I do?* I wondered.

"Tell him about the pink ribbon," came the reply.

I didn't know anything about pink ribbons but when I asked my Magical Question that always gave me the perfect answer, I got a great idea!

I invited Nicky to play a special game with me. I placed three chairs in a little triangle and asked Nicky to sit on one. I sat on the second and I asked him to pretend his daddy was sitting on the third chair.

"Can you imagine your daddy here, Nicky?" I asked.

He nodded his head up and down several times.

"Good." I continued, "Nicky, there is a very special LOVE that wants to be with you and your daddy right now. It is more powerful than any LOVE you've ever known before!

"This special LOVE loves you when you cannot LOVE yourself. It knows everything about you, about everyone, about everything in the world! It even knows all the answers to your tests in school.

It gives you the courage to say yes or no when it is best and gives you joy, kindness, patience, wisdom and so much more! It is everything!

"It is not human LOVE, it is God's LOVE!

"If you could give that LOVE a color, it would be pink. Now, close your eyes and imagine a wonderful pink ribbon of LOVE floating down, down, down from Heaven.

"Pretend one end of the pink ribbon is slowly entering the top of your head, moving down, down, down and out your heart.

The other end of the floats over to your dad and stops at the top of his head. Ask your daddy if he wants your ribbon because, no one, not even God, can force him to take it if he doesn't want it; everyone has free will, and can choose to accept or not. Does your daddy want your gift?"

Nicky quickly nodded his head up and down.

"Great" I continued, "pretend it is going in the top of his head, slowly coming down, down, down and out his heart. The two loose ends are floating towards each other. Who is going to tie the two loose ends together to make a knot?" I asked.

My mouth was saying the words yet, my mind was thinking, *Caroline, what do you expect him to say; he hasn't spoken in three months!*

Clearly, without hesitation, Nicky replied, "I will, but my daddy will help me cuz I'm not very good with knots."

He had spoken a full sentence, clearly, without any problem! I had goose bumps and got a tad teary eyed. I had to get in control of my feelings!

I whispered, "Nicky, this pink ribbon is very special. It's magical. It's mystical. It cannot be cut. It cannot be burned. It never wears out and it stretches! You are now connected to your daddy until the end of time with this gift of LOVE. Nothing can break that connection!

"Whenever you miss your daddy, just think of the pink ribbon in your heart and at that exact moment, no matter where he is, even if you're an old man and your daddy's died and gone to heaven, he will begin thinking of you and feel that special LOVE coming from you to him. The LOVE that LOVEs you when you cannot LOVE yourself."

"Really?" he asked as a tear rolled down his cheek.

I prayed for a sign that I had done the right thing.

At that exact moment, his grandmother knocked on my door and said, "Nicky, come quick! Your father's on the phone long distance."

Nicky blasted out of my apartment into his grandmother's.

"I was just thinking about you," Nicky's dad said.

"I know" Nicky squealed with delight, "I just sent you a pink ribbon!"

Nicky's dad had no idea what he was talking about but he knew something special had happened because Nicky was talking perfectly!

His grandmother and father were in shock yet totally thrilled.

Since then LOVE has inspired Nicky to share pink ribbons with everyone, even with those who have died.

The first time someone did say "No" to Nicky, he was very confused. It was his little cousin Suzie who was always sick. After months of testing, the doctors still didn't know why she was sick.

By now Nicky knew LOVE could heal so before he went to sleep he thought of her and mentally sent her a pink ribbon.

It went in his head, out his heart and the other end floated out of his house, across the city, through the roof of Suzie's house into her bedroom and stopped on top of her head. When he asked Suzie if she wanted his pink ribbon, in his mind he heard her say, "No."

Nicky didn't understand however, he knew LOVE would know why she was refusing it. When he asked LOVE why Suzie didn't want his gift, LOVE gave him the idea Suzie's dad, who worked at home, was always too busy to spend time with her unless she was sick.

That's why she didn't want the pink ribbon, it would make her feel better and she wouldn't get the LOVE and attention she so desperately wanted from her daddy. She was missing him.

Nicky now knew why the doctors couldn't find anything wrong with her.

He let her end of the pink ribbon float down to her feet and forgot about it. Her heart and soul would pick it up when she was ready.

Her heart must have picked it up while she slept because she woke up the next morning feeling much better! Suzie and her mom were visiting the next day. She looked so much healthier and happier.

Nicky told Suzie about LOVE'S MAGICAL CONNECTION and helped her connect with her father. That special LOVE worked its magic on Suzie's Dad because he began stopping his work to spend time with her just when she needed it without her getting sick first.

Nicky also shared pink ribbons with groups, using one ribbon, in the head and out the heart, of each person until the last person accepted it and then tied the knot.

If a person in a group said, "No" he left that person out and continued to the next one.

He noticed that the person left out would, sooner or later, pop into his mind and seem to ask for his or her own connection, wanting to be included.

He shared a pink ribbon with his hockey team, then his classmates and the people in his apartment block, wherever LOVE moved him to do so. Sometimes he was surprised to see who would tie the knot.

When he began sharing LOVE's gift with someone who was mean to him, something special would happen; that person started changing and acting nicer. Some even became his good friends.

Nicky knows he just has to think about a pink ribbon and, there it is ... because LOVE never runs out.

He also knows he must silently ask permission first. If he thinks the person is saying, "No" he still imagines one end of the pink ribbon going in through the top of his head and out his heart and then he lets the other end of the ribbon float down to that person's feet and forgets about it.

Although this was happening just in his mind and heart, it began changing his life and that of those he shared it with. Nicky has not been the same since and that was in 1982.

LOVE ASKS ...

1. Who do you want to share a pink ribbon with?

2. How did it make you feel?

3. Did you notice a change in the person you shared it with?

You cannot get through a single day
without having an impact
on the world around you.
What you do makes a difference,
and you have to decide
what kind of difference
you want to make.

~ Jane Goodall ~
https://www.biography.com/people/jane-goodall-9542363

LOVE'S GIFT HEALS DEATH WISH
~ The Power of LOVE ~

"I want to die," cried eight-year-old Jane. "I want to be with Grandpa so I can help him."

Jane's grandpa had died a year before. She dreamed about him every night and he always looked so sick.

For a year, her priest and psychiatrist could not talk her out of wanting to die, so her mother brought her to me. I'm often the last resort people go to.

I told her about LOVE'S MAGICAL CONNECTION and when it was time to have Jane mentally offer a pink ribbon to her grandpa, LOVE gave me the idea that she should close her eyes and remember what he looked like when he was his sickest.

"Oh," she whispered sadly, "he's in the hospital. He's so skinny and weak and he smells awful. He has so many tubes in him."

I asked her to imagine LOVE's wonderful pink ribbon floating down in through her head and out her heart as Nicky had. Then it floated over to her grandpa's head.

"Does he want your gift of LOVE?" I asked. "Oh, yes!" Jane said excitedly.

"Good. See it go in the top of his head and come out his heart," I continued. "Now, who is going to tie the two loose ends to make a knot?" I asked.

"Grandma!" Jane answered very surprised. "How can that be? She died before Grandpa did!"

"It's all perfect," I answered. "Trust LOVE. It knows exactly who you need at this time.

You are now connected, until the end of time, to your grandpa with that special LOVE. Whenever you miss him just think of the pink ribbon in your heart and no matter where he is, he will feel it.

"Now watch what happens after the knot is tied."

A few moments later she began getting excited. "Oh! He looks better! The tubes are coming out! He's putting on weight! He now smells like the Brut aftershave I gave him for Christmas. He's getting out of bed and moving around! He's picking me up and dancing with me!"

Tears of joy were coming down Jane's face as she was imagining this scene in her mind.

"Wonderful," I said. "Now your Grandpa is going to set you on his lap and whisper something very important in your ear, something you need to hear. What does he say?"

"Oh! He's telling me that I have already helped him. It is not my time to go where he is. I'll be an old lady when it's my time and he will be the first one to meet me! He is going to help me help all my friends who are missing their grandmas and grandpas. He will send me words and ideas down the pink ribbon to tell them so they can feel better too. How wonderful!"

Jane no longer talks about dying and is now a wonderful inspiration to young and old alike.

You, dear reader, are invited to share a pink ribbon with anyone and everyone; however, don't forget, you must have permission first.

Remember, even though it is only in your imagination, it works!

If you have any doubt if someone wants it just place your gift of LOVE at his or her feet. The heart knows when to pick it up.

Some people cannot visualize easily or even imagine. If you are one of those, just pretend. LOVE is more powerful than your inabilities.

It will do the work necessary to connect you to your loved one because LOVE wants oneness, connections, LOVE for all.

The person you are sharing a pink ribbon with may begin to think about you and begin to feel warm and fuzzy inside at that exact moment.

Don't stop at just one person, share LOVE's pink ribbon with as many people as you can, even groups of people, in the head and out the heart of each person.

The supply is endless.

LOVE ASKS ...

1. Which person in the spirit world do you want a Magical Connection with?

2. What special message does that person want to tell you?

3. What question would you like to ask him or her? Do so now. Trust the first thoughts, feelings, ideas, pictures you get.

LOVE USES THE CHILDREN
~ They Teach The Teacher ~

"Do you do workshops for children?" a parent asked.

"Why?" I asked.

"Well my son is seeing things no one else sees in his room and I think you're the only one who can help him," she replied.

Although I had run day care centers, playground and teen programs while in the military, it wasn't the same as a metaphysical workshop. I had conducted them for teens and adults, covering everything from angels, healing, guides, death, suicide, dreams and more; however, for kids I wasn't so sure I was qualified.

I had made a pact with God and LOVE many years prior, *If you want me to do something I have to hear the request three times.*

The following week a teacher asked if I conducted spiritual workshops for children. When I asked why she replied, "I have a boy in my class who keeps talking about having been here before in a past life, which doesn't go over too well in a Catholic school. I know you deal with past lives and I know you can help him.

"His parents believe in reincarnation but don't know how to help him. The child is being called a liar by the other kids and he's starting to have a lot of problems," she concluded.

That was two!

That night a call from the boy's parents requesting a workshop made it the third request. If you can get me at least six other children with their parents' permission I will conduct one," I told the parent fearfully. I was beginning to think LOVE had more faith and trust in me than I had.

Ten kids between the ages of four and fourteen arrived, bright – eyed and ready to work and play Saturday morning.

The two teenagers wanted to be childcare workers when they graduated from high school so I made them my junior helpers.

All morning long, we danced and sang and did a lot of specialized exercises that would balance their energy and ground them. We didn't talk about energy as such, we were just having fun. I was the only one who knew about energy … or so I thought.

After lunch everyone was ready to do some quiet work. I gave them their art supplies that included a notebook for each child. On the cover I had written, The Masters of the Universe Workshop … A Refresher Course for Old Souls in Young Bodies. The kids loved the title and loved being 'masters of the universe' like the animated heroes on TV.

Oops! Can't call a workshop that name again. I don't want to get sued. I didn't even know there was such a TV show.

I had never done a metaphysical workshop for little ones, so I needed to put my trust entirely in the guidance LOVE was giving me.

"What do you want us to do in our books?" asked four-year-old Jeff.

What would LOVE tell them? I wondered. Suddenly, "I want you to draw a picture of God" came out of my mouth. I was surprised. I had not mentioned God once all morning. I didn't want to get into anything that might sound religious. *What will they draw? How can anyone draw God?*

"I can't draw," Jeff let me know.

"That's Ok, Jeff. Let God draw God." That response also caught me by surprise!

"Oh, Ok," he said as he got to work. Within five minutes they were all finished and shared their work with the class.

"Is your God a star?" I asked Jeff as he held up his picture.

"Well," he began, "God is in a star; but that's not a star! Don't you know what God is?"

"What?" I asked excitedly, wondering what he would say.

"God is energy!"

"And what does your God love to do the most?" I asked humbly.

Jeff lifted his head, rolled up his eyes and sighed, "Oh, my God loves to think and every time He thinks, poof, there it is!"

I was in my forties just learning that and here was a four-year-old who remembered!

Six-year-old Sara drew a tree, "Use me. Re-use me. Don't abuse me," was her message.

Fourteen-year-old Tina drew the light at the end of the tunnel; "To be or not to be, that is the question" was her message.

Five-year-old Samuel drew a stick man with a clown suit.

"Is your God a clown?" I chuckled.

Sam laughed, "Don't you remember? Sound is the first thing that was created. We must laugh and sing every day."

Out of the mouths of babes! In my teens, I would have drawn an old man with a white beard and a stick at the top of the mountain.

I didn't have to worry about being qualified to teach these children. All I had to do was listen to them as they were teaching me. LOVE knew exactly which children to send me so I could learn to listen, trust, and serve all ages.

That was the first of many workshops I have conducted with young children and teens.

As a result, THE FIREFLY FLIGHT BOOK – A METAPHYSICAL WORKBOOK FOR KIDS AGED 2 TO 200 - my one-week workshop in workbook form was written to help parents and teachers guide the youth of today often referred to as Indigo or Crystal children.

LOVE ASKS …

1. What does of picture of God look like to you?

2. How many times do you need to hear something before you to take action?

3. Have you noticed how gifted today's children are?

We are what we repeatedly do;
excellence, then,
is not an act but a habit.

~ Aristotle ~
https://www.biography.com/people/aristotle-9188415

LOVE BLESSES THE CHILD
~ LOVE Can Be Scary ~

"I don't want to go to bed," three-year-old Samuel cried. "Those people are in my room again!"

"Are they the same people?" asked his mom.

"Ya! That man and woman and the boy. The man is going to hit the boy with a stick." He cried, unable to stop shaking.

"Ok, you can sleep with Johnny again" she said, trying to calm him down. *I need to get some help,* she thought. *Three weeks of this is enough!*

I was called because I worked with troubled/gifted children; knew what to say to them; and, because Samuel knew me.

His aunt had dabbled in black magic and his mother wondered if she had left some negative energy around that Samuel could see. She and Sam's dad were separated and were headed for divorce. She had to move to a troubled part of town where Samuel witnessed child abuse more than once.

"Maybe he is just stressed out because of the divorce and seeing his little friend get hit by his dad with a stick," his mom told me on the phone, trying to convince herself.

We chatted for a short while and I ended the call with, "I will see you tomorrow when I get in town,"

I told her. "Try to get some sleep. I know everything is going to be ok."

I knew she really believed it was negative energy. It took me eight hours to travel by bus.

My mind tried to repeat every negative black magic story I had ever heard or read about. I wouldn't allow it. I kept reminding myself that we were all loved and protected by the greatest power of all - LOVE. Mind you, I had no idea what I was going to do or say when I got there.

Samuel ran to me to give me a big hug as soon as I arrived. I hadn't even taken off my coat when he began telling me about his problem.

"There are people in my room every time I try to sleep," he said.

"The man is going to hit me. I'm scared. Bobby got hurt by his daddy."

I had to think quickly. I could feel his fear. *What would LOVE say?* "I have an idea, Samuel," I began. "What if we put a picture on the wall in your room?"

"What good is that?" he asked.

"Well, when these people show up you tell them, 'Hi. I am tired and it is time for me to go to sleep. If you want to talk to someone you talk to the people in the picture.'"

Yeah right! Like a picture is going to do it? I thought.

"Good idea," he said as he gave me a hug and took off to play.

Thank God I didn't listen to my human self.

I had traveled eight hours to say a few words! I hadn't even taken my coat off and I was finished! His fear was gone. I was at least staying for supper! lol

After the boys went to bed in Johnny's room, there was a long discussion about which picture to use. A picture of Brother Andre, who was a family favorite because he had healed the grandfather, was suggested.

LOVE said, "No." It didn't feel right for me. No decision had been reached before I left for my return journey home.

"You will know it when you see it," I said. "Call me when you do."

Two weeks later I got a call that still gives me shivers, humbles me and explains why people always talk about the light around Samuel.

His mom began telling me, "My mom remembered a big old picture in her attic and felt it was perfect.

"When I was putting it up, Samuel started screaming, "Don't put that picture up! That's the people I see in my room every night!'

It was a picture of the Holy family, the child Jesus, Mary and Joseph with his staff (stick). Samuel didn't know who these people were, so he feared them.

A simple but brief explanation removed his fear enabling him to sleep in peace in his room once more.

He is one of many gifted children on this planet to do special work. He has been and still is a channel of healing energy for many and the Holy Family is obviously part of his team of helpers.

Samuel is now in his thirties. His laughter, joy, music and enthusiastic zest for life, and all it has to offer, continue to inspire and touch people's hearts, bringing out the best in them.

At moments like this I feel so blessed to have been a part of helping one of LOVE's Earth Angels. Again, LOVE revealed the truth that made no sense to my human self but was perfect for the child.

LOVE ASKS ...

1. Were you ever afraid of boogey men in your room as a child?

2. Did you ever see someone ... others did not see?

3. What picture would you put up on your wall for inspiration and protection?

LOVE USES SAM
~ The Power of A Child ~

"There is a Reiki course coming up and I think we should offer it to Sam," Mom suggested.

Four-year-old Samuel had already demonstrated natural healing abilities and often said, "Don't ask me to do that," when asked to send energy to someone sick. "I know what to do and when to do it."

Is it in his highest interest to bring more attention to him? Will this cause extra pressure on one so young? I wondered. I asked, *What would LOVE do?* and heard, "Let him choose."

Samuel decided to take the course and was the only child amongst the twelve students on the course. He fit in perfectly despite his age and size. There were times the instructor knew Samuel wished he were outside playing with his friends and was amazed that the boy did not complain.

Reiki is a healing technique that allows universal energy to flow through a body to help it have peace and release stress, thereby allowing the body to heal itself.

In Reiki 1st Degree, the facilitator places his or her hands on twelve body positions and holds them for five minutes each, taking an hour to do a session. Because it was an exercise to practice, the students were not required to hold each position for the full five minutes.

"I want you to get a partner and hold the back positions," the students were told.

Samuel found his partner. She practiced first and when it was his turn to give, Samuel stood on a chair to reach her shoulder blades in Back Position No. 1.

"Move to position No. 2," they were instructed. Sam's left hand slid down lower to the proper position, but his right stayed where it was.

The instructor knew of Samuel's natural gift so he observed and allowed Sam to do what he was moved to do.

"Move to position No.3," came the next instruction.

Again Samuel's left hand moved down and his right hand stayed put. The instructor continued to watch what Sam was doing and just let him be.

"Move to the last position," was the final instruction. By now Samuel was looking a little bored as was eyeing the kids outside. He smiled his silly grin and began giggling when he saw the instructor watching him.

Finally, it was over. Everyone sat down and began to share their experience. Within a few moments, Samuel's partner began sobbing.

"Is something wrong?" the instructor asked.

"Wrong? No! Everything is right! Look at me!" she squealed with delight, making bigger and bigger circles with her right arm. She couldn't stop crying and laughing!

"I haven't been able to lift my arm for three years," she sobbed, "and now I can move it freely and with no pain!"

Her right shoulder had been blocked and in pain with bursitis for three years. A few minutes with Samuel and Reiki erased all of that.

"Can I go out to play now?" he asked.

Everyone laughed as he ran out the door. Did LOVE ask us to offer the course because Samuel needed it or was it because LOVE knew Samuel's partner was ready for a wonderful healing, knowing Samuel's childlike innocence and Reiki could do the job?

LOVE ASKS ...

1. Have you ever had a Reiki session?

2. Do you believe children can heal others?

3. Do you believe YOU can heal others?

*It is of practical value to learn
to like yourself.
Since you must spend so much time
with yourself
you might as well get some satisfaction
out of the relationship.*

~ Norman Vincent Peale ~
https://www.youtube.com/watch?v=uFGZf899fzw

LOVE REMINDS US
~ Just Ask ~

"Jessica is dying. It isn't fair! She's only six-years-old!" cried her mother, Joan. "It doesn't make sense. How could she be full of cancer?"

Jessica's grandmother was visiting. She listened and tried to comfort her but didn't know how to answer. Both were unaware that Jessica's friend, four-year-old Samuel was listening.

"Do you want me to say a prayer for her?" he asked.

"Yes, that would be nice," Joan replied, surprised a child so young would ask that.

One month later Joan was telling everyone that little Jessica was in remission and was doing well. The doctors couldn't explain it.

LOVE and Samuel were a dynamite team. It wasn't the first time he had asked If he could help or pray for someone.

I was wondering what he did, felt, saw, thought, or said when he was 'praying'. I personally had learned many healing techniques and knew there were as many ways to heal, as there were healers.

I was thinking about Samuel and his abilities when LOVE's little voice whispered, "Ask him what he does." So I did.

"Samuel, what do you do exactly when you send healing energies to someone like Jessica? Do you pray, send colors, sounds, words, visualize? What do you do?"

"Don't you remember the story you told us? The Secret of The Magic Eye," he asked. "That's what I use."

I remembered telling him, his two-year-old brother, and three - year - old cousin the story. It was totally inspired and had told it only once so, I wasn't sure what part he remembered.

"What part do you remember, Samuel that helps you heal?" I asked.

"You told us that God made us all perfect and that some of us have forgotten how perfect we are, so I put my hands under my pillow," he continued, "and when they get hot I say, 'God Bless Mommy. God Bless Daddy and by the way Jessica forgot how perfect she is; will You remind her?' Then I go to sleep."

Ask and you shall receive. By the way, Jessica is alive and well, cancer free and the mother of a sweet little boy!

LOVE ASKS ...

1. Do YOU believe all you have to do is ask?

2. Can you believe that a child born with physical disabilities is perfect?

3. Are you willing to try asking again and trusting and believing as Sam did?

Life is a succession of lessons
which must be lived
to be understood.

~ Helen Keller ~
https://www.biography.com/people/helen-keller-9361967

LOVE TELLS YOU WHY I'M DIFFERENT
~ Don't Judge A Book By Its Cover ~

Joe and Sally attended my healing workshop in Ottawa, Ontario, Canada and were very pleased with their results. They asked if I would be able to spend some time with their daughter who was having trouble in school.

Nancy was a 15-year-old mentally challenged child in a public grade school attending classes at grade 4 and 5 levels. Her parents believed if they sent her to a special needs school she would regress even more. The kids in school were calling her a dummy and a retard. She bit all her fingernails and toenails until they bled and was getting into fights.

I agreed to try.

They traveled from Ottawa to Kingston, where I lived and after we chatted a bit and Nancy was comfortable we began. Her parents had asked for permission to record our conversation so she could listen to it when at home, hoping she would get some inspiration from it.

"Why do you bite your nails?" I asked;

"Duh, I don't know," she replied.

"Why do you think the kids in school make fun of you?"

"Duh, I don't know."

After the fourth, "Duh, I don't know" I knew I wasn't getting anywhere.

I began to wonder, *What would LOVE do?* and felt myself begin to shudder and shift and feel really nasty and ugly inside. Suddenly I was spewing, "No wonder everybody calls you a dummy and a retard," I said, "You keep saying, 'Duh, I don't know.' If I heard that all the time I would call you a dummy and a retard too."

Oh my God! What's happening? I never spoke like that to anyone, especially someone with special needs!

If anything, I tended to be extremely compassionate and understanding.

The parents were in shock, as was I. I had no idea what was going to come out of my mouth next ... and a tape recorder was recording the whole thing! Even though I was aware of the parents' concerns and could feel Nancy withdraw I continued. "I thought you said God was inside you?"

"Uh-huh," she whispered.

"Good," I replied sternly. "From this moment on I don't want to hear another word from you!"

I had another sudden shift and began to feel my usual self. Gently, I continued, "I want you to let God use your tongue, your throat, your teeth, your breath, and mind. I want you to let God do all the talking."

"Ok," she whispered. I asked her to breathe deeply in through the nose and out through the mouth three times. When she relaxed I began asking her questions.

For fifteen minutes she spoke clearly in three and four-syllable words with no hesitation, answering every question asked, telling us why she chose her mother, why she chose her father. They would provide her with the support and nurturing she needed to do her work.

When I asked the next question, we were not ready for her reply. "Why did your soul choose a body that would look and act retarded?"

"That's so simple," she replied with a gentle smile, "I came to teach LOVE. It is easy for you to LOVE me when I look like you and talk like you and walk like you. But will you still LOVE me when I drool, chew my nails until they bleed, when you have to change my diaper? I came to teach LOVE."

A sacred hush filled the room. I couldn't speak. Tears filled my eyes then as they do every time I share Nancy's story. Her true beauty and grace just took my breath away. The tape recorder clicked off a few seconds later.

Nancy and her parents left my home that day with big smiles on their faces and hearts filled with peace.

Nancy now knew why her soul chose to 'act' retarded and graciously accepted her role. She came to teach us LOVE.

Two months later I got a card from Nancy's mom saying Nancy was going for her first professional manicure … God did not want to chew fingernails anymore.

She was also much happier because the other girls were now inviting her to join them in their games.

Why the change?

Before she was projecting the thought, the echo, "Nobody likes me," so the universe, LOVE, was required to obey her creative free will and had to send her people to call her names and to reject her. The echo ALWAYS comes back, multiplied.

Now she was projecting the thought, the echo, "I am here to teach LOVE." Knowing that changed her energy, gave her confidence and filled her with self-esteem, which in turn, made the others like her more. They were the echo returning to her multiplied.

This experience was truly humbling yet, very frightening for me. I had never acted so harshly with anyone before. LOVE must have known what Nancy, I and her parents needed, to do our life's work.

We all now knew why LOVE and Nancy chose to be 'different.'

LOVE ASKS ...

1. Do you know any special needs children?

2. Do you now see how they are absolutely perfect for their mission?

3. Do you think YOU could be a parent, a caregiver, for one so special?

You may find the worst enemy or best friend in yourself.

~ English Proverb ~

LOVE KNOWS HOW TO LISTEN
~ Teen Saves Her Friend's Life ~

"Caroline, it happened exactly as you said in class last week," 15year-old Lois shared excitedly.

"Would you like to share it with the class?" I asked hoping it would jog my memory.

"I went to Tim Horton's for coffee and donut with Sara. She was going to tell me about her hot date with this hunk. I wanted to hear all the juicy details because I have a crush on the guy too.

"As soon as Sara started speaking I spaced out. I went blank. In the past I would have shaken myself and thought, 'Pay attention to your friend. Listen to her.' But I remembered what you taught us in class; that LOVE does not waste energy. It sends us exactly what we need when we need it for whatever reason.

"The only thing in my mind was the image of a hand making a downward motion. I mentally asked, '*Ok LOVE what does this mean?*' and I immediately remembered the one and only time my father gave me a pat on my bum when I was six-years-old. I was puzzled and still felt like a space cadet.

"All of a sudden I could hear her voice in the distance and I panicked! I had to say something to look like I had been paying attention! I wondered, *what would LOVE say?*

"When she stopped speaking I was surprised at what came out of my mouth, "To change the subject, how are things at home?"

It had nothing to do with our conversation!

Sara began sobbing. "My dad's been beating me. I've been thinking about killing myself," she replied.

Sara had not showing any of the outward signs of suicide. Because Lois knew how to listen, she was able to get both Sara and her father some much needed help. LOVE sure knew how to bait this hook. "Let's go talk about the guys" and once hooked, LOVE knew it could use Lois to help a friend in need.

WoW! It sure must have been a wonderful class I taught last week! Umm ... wonder what LOVE wants me to share this week? I chuckled.

LOVE ASKS ...

1. Do you space out when someone is talking to you?

2. Do you think LOVE is wanting to use you at that moment?

3. When is the last time, your hook was baited to do something and you ended up doing something totally different only to find out it was perfect, exactly what was needed?

CONTRIBUTORS

YOU CAN DO THE SAME

AS I

AND EVEN MORE!

~ Jesus ~

Jean Lafleur, Fern Rancourt
and
Diana Holloway

Tried and were successful!

How About You?

You don't inspire your teammates
by showing them
how amazing you are.

You inspire them
by showing them
how amazing they are.

~ Robyn Benincasa ~
http://premierespeakers.com/robyn_benincasa/bio

LOVE INSPIRES THE TEACHER
~ She Remembers The Basics ~
Jean Lafleur

I had been teaching spiritual and personal development courses for several years before this particular group came to me. Normally classes on this subject attracted women, not men.

It was obvious the energies of society and the planet were shifting because I had three men in this class of seven. These dynamic students were like sponges, eagerly applying all they learned, wanting to test everything so they could eventually trust what I taught.

We were into the seventh week of the 12-week course when I sensed a change. *Was it a lack of interest? Had they outgrown the material or the teacher already?*

I had to admit they absorbed everything more quickly than any class I had ever taught before. I was beginning to doubt myself.

"I won't be here next week," John said sheepishly on his way out the door when the class was over.

"Neither will I," echoed Marc.

"I won't be here either," yelled Lise as they went out the door.

Now I was really troubled. My feelings were being confirmed. They didn't really give a reason for not attending.

I followed them out to the parking lot and noticed they were all stuck waiting for the traffic to clear.

I felt I had to address the issue before they left but wasn't sure how to do it so I thought, *What would LOVE do?* and immediately remembered something I had learned at the beginning of my own journey that was so simple and basic I often forgot about it ... "Ask for divine order in this situation" came the reply.

I quickly ran to my students and told them, "If you want the traffic to clear ask for divine order in the traffic. You'll see it will clear up. Try it," I suggested.

They all looked at me and chuckled but gave it a try. Within seconds the traffic cleared and they were off. I had no idea how that was going to solve my dilemma about attendance but I thought, *Well, LOVE, I did as you suggested. The rest is up to you.*

Much to my surprise I had a full class the following week. They were all buzzing about divine order and how it moved things for them, made things happen so quickly.

"I asked for divine order when my car wouldn't start and bingo it started!" said one.

"I asked for divine order with my mother and me because we're always fighting and we had a peaceful week," said another.

John added, "I didn't think there was much more to learn in this class and didn't plan on coming back. But when you told us about divine order and it worked, Jean, I knew the lessons were just beginning.

I asked for divine order in my feelings about this class and here I am. Sock it to me Jean, teach me more."

I don't know why I was surprised but I was. LOVE in its wisdom wanted me to remember how simple yet powerful and basic LOVE was, still teaching the teacher.

LOVE ASKS ...

1. Have you ever thought of quitting just to find out, you were just getting started?

2. Would you consider asking for Divine Order in your life?

3. Would it freak you out if Divine Order started creating miracles for you?

Ask yourself three questions.

The first, what comes easy to me but harder to others?

The second question is, what would I do for work for years and years and never have to get paid for it?

The third question is, how can I be of service and how can I give back?

Because I always say, 'If you're here on Earth and you're not living on the edge, you're taking up too much room."

~ Farrah Gray ~
http://abcnews.go.com/2020/Business/story?id=2247424&page=1

LOVE'S HERO
~ The Child's And The Woman's ~
Jean Lafleur

The "Stranger With Scrolls Becomes Hero For A Day" headline caught my eye.

A street person's simple but very time-consuming act inspired the journalist to have a contest to find other heroes in our community. The contest tweaked my imagination as I wondered who my hero could be.

Who would LOVE pick, I wondered. It was the easiest question to answer. I instantly knew! A couple of hours later my story was written and submitted to our local paper the next day.

The year 1928 was a time of great poverty for many. That's the year I was born, the baby in a family of one boy and five girls, all very close in age. My father did his best to find work but had to swallow his pride often and go on relief when he couldn't pay the rent; it often meant we had to move.

Food was more important than toys so we learned to do without play things. Mom's tired hands patiently transformed flour and sugar bags into simple dresses, which made us the butt of cruel jokes at school.

We spoke broken French at home but went to English schools because that's all there was in those days.

I often froze my feet and hands walking three miles to school in the winter. It's no wonder I LOVE long summer walks today.

Christmases past were not like today's. One year Mom and Dad were able to buy us a doll ... one doll for five girls! That was the beginning of our fights.

"That doll is no good if it makes you fight," Mom and Dad said, taking it away, never to be seen again.

How I dreamed of having my very own beautiful doll! I prayed that someday someone would LOVE me enough to buy me one.

"I am going to have a doll someday," I told my sisters. They just laughed and laughed. That made me dream more and more.

When I was nine years old Dad came home with that look on his face that said, "It's time to move." This time we're moving to Quebec! I panicked! Quebec! French schools! What do I know about French? Nothing! It was awful!

Again we were laughed at. Again I was an outsider. Again I dreamed of my doll, of someone loving me.

Quebec had one good point, my mom's brother, Uncle Jean, whom we had never met before. After we settled in, he invited me for a visit.

"Come in little one," he said to me when I arrived, "I have something to give you.

"My mother made this for my little girl a long time ago but your aunt and I had only boys. I was never able to give it to someone till now. I believe you are that special little girl I was supposed to give it to."

Before my eyes appeared the most beautiful doll I had ever seen. I cried and cried and cried and cried. I couldn't stop crying. My dream had come true! Someone DOES love me! I AM special!

As precious as that doll was it was never as precious as my Uncle Jean became to me in that instant. I still cry thinking of that moment; the first time I met a hero, my hero, Uncle Jean.

That doll and I became inseparable; it became my security blanket, reminding me how special and loved I was when the rest of the world told me the opposite. Uncle Jean continued touching my heart with his warmth, kindness, and gentle ways throughout my young life.

I am eighty-four years of age today and my hero left this earth a long, long time ago. I still shed tears when I think of him, tears of joy for having been blessed as his little girl and tears of longing to see him again when my time comes. I hope he'll be one of the first ones to meet me.

I can't wait to tell him how much of a hero he was to a frightened little girl many years ago and still is to the older woman today.

As I wrote this story I realized, for the first time, why I LOVE buying and giving away dolls, all kinds of dolls, to all kinds of people, pretty ones, ugly ones, broken or whole!

I want to give others the same feeling of LOVE and acceptance my hero gave me!

Oh, my God! Another realization just hit me. That's why I like the broken ones best! I can fix them like my hero fixed me. It also explained why so many children and adults that I have given a doll to run up to hug me to this day ... I guess I have become a hero to them.

I am so thankful to LOVE for helping me realize how my hero made an impact on me and helped me win the contest, which has inspired others to be more accepting of those without.

LOVE ASKS ...

1. Are YOU someone's hero?

2. Why? What did you do or say to earn that title?

3. Why not find a way to be a hero for someone, every day?

LOVE GOES TO TIBET
~ It's Easier Than You Think ~
Jean Lafleur

"Do you want to go on a fantastic trip to Tibet?" my daughter asked me all excited, hardly able to contain herself.

"Tibet! Oh my! I don't have money for a trip like that," I replied.

"You can do it," she continued. "You have eight months. Just tell the universe if it wants you to go to send you the money and you will go. You will have it before you know it."

The saving began. My students and customers knew of my dream and were excited for me. Everyone began leaving donations in the 3-foot-high Coke bottle bank in my office. I was getting excited.

Four months later I decided to find out how much money was in my bank. I counted seven hundred and eighty-five dollars! I could hardly believe it! I had enough to believe it was possible. Now I was really excited!

I had already begun the preparations necessary for a trip to the top of the world; the breathing, meditating, and physical exercises necessary to make sure I would stay healthy. I was going to Tibet! To the top of the world in the Himalayan mountains!

Our group was to meet the Dalai Lama in Dharmsala, India.

This was definitely a trip of a lifetime and to make it really special one of my students was also going.

Two months later I went to count my money again. *What the? The bottle is empty! No, it can't be! I must have put it away somewhere to hide it.* I looked and looked and cried and cried till all hope was lost.

I remembered my daughter always telling me when stuck to ask, *What would LOVE do?* So I asked.

"Ask for divine order in this situation and be open to someone lending you the money," came the thought.

Are my thoughts playing tricks on me? Who would or could lend me over a thousand dollars? My despair was so deep. My students were almost as depressed as I was.

Half an hour before my next class was about to begin, the student also planning to go to Tibet said she had to speak to me.

"If you don't go to Tibet that means I am not supposed to go either," she shared.

"I was told in my meditation to lend you the money to go if you wish. You can pay it back interest free when you have it."

Her husband had just inherited some money making it was possible for her to be so generous.

The money was offered and with some shyness I accepted. It was such a gift! Off to India, Nepal, and Tibet we went. Never to be the same again!

That experience changed my life in many ways. From that moment on I grew to trust LOVE more and more.

It would never give me the desire to do something and then not send me what I need to accomplish it.

I was so glad I had LOVE on my team. I was kept very busy with more customers than usual upon my return, making it easy to pay my debt off.

LOVE ASKS ...

1. Have you ever lost anything that was REALLY valuable?

2. How did you react?

3. Would you have been comfortable accepting the money as Jean did?

We do not need magic
to transform our world.
We carry all the power we need
inside ourselves already.
We have the power to imagine better.

~ J.K. Rowling ~
https://www.biography.com/people/jk-rowling-40998

LOVE'S TREE AND ME
~ Now I Understand ~
Jean Lafleur

I have always felt awe looking at trees and wondered why they touched me the way they did. During one of my many strolls through a wooded area near camp I sat on a rock and looked at one of my favorites and as I was filled with LOVE I asked LOVE why this tree was so special.

The following poem gently flowed out of my heart into my conscious mind; shifted and spun the whole thing around until I found we are the same, we are one. The tree's thoughts will be in a different font for easy reading…

THE TREE

I am little and six sitting under a tree
Loving the tall tall being looming high over me.
I look at the tree and it looks back at me!

Do you like looking at me?
Do you like what you see?

Yes, of course I do," I giggle with glee,
Cause when I look at you I am looking at me!

How can that be? I'm so different from you!

My father is tall just like you.
Your white bark wraps around like
mother's arms around me.

275

You swing your branches like I swing on my porch.
Right now, I feel quite good, how about you?

Usually I do, but not today.
Someone cut me, tore at my skin,
how cruel some can be!

Yes, I understand pain.
Remember when I fell off you?

Oh yes, I remember, it made me so blue!

Oh, please don't cry, your sap will become dry
I Loved climbing high on you,
I almost touched the sky!

I begin to see that you're truly like me!
See that tree over there - my sister's grandson.
He's dying so young …
and he's not the only one!

I'm so sorry for your pain, I have mine too.
I have cancer, losing my hair, getting chemo too.
I must believe I'll get fit; I've so much to do.

I can see now, how we're so much alike.
We must stop, look and listen

Oh, God is so smart. He made us so perfect,
the tall and the small.
Loving us equally, trees, children and all.

I must leave and thank you my friend,
You've taken my pain away.

Tell your friends to come visit,
I will look at them too.
We will look at each other the way you and I do.

Let's go on loving and pass it on.
It will heal our pain ...
And remind us We are One.

LOVE ASKS ...

1. Do you believe trees have feelings and thoughts?

2. Have you ever carved your initials into a tree?

3. How do you feel when trees are cut down leaving the land bare?

Great spirits have always encountered violent opposition from mediocre minds.

~ Albert Einstein
~https://www.nobelprize.org/nobel_prizes/physics/laureates/1921/ einstein-bio.html

LOVE'S MOVING WORDS
~ I Am Forced To Grow ~
Diana Holloway

"I don't LOVE you anymore." George said quietly. The room moved beneath my feet. I couldn't comprehend the words. The words I would hear for years to come whirled about madly in my head.

"I don't LOVE you anymore. I'm sorry. That's just the way it is. I have to leave."

How foolish I had been to trust and love him! I was now left alone to face life and to move forward, attempting to move towards my destiny, whatever that was. I had to learn to face the challenge and begin to live. I was always told I was a late bloomer.

God! I cried out, *I know You LOVE me. If there is one that's me, I know it is You. I am part of You. Please tell me what You want me to do. What would LOVE want me to do?*

I sensed I had to wait for something. Two weeks went by. LOVE's call finally came, a call from a former vocal teacher whom I had not spoken to in ten years.

"Diana, I want to meet you for lunch," she said.

My curiosity got the best of me so we met the next day. She looked at me with that knowing look teachers have.

"I know you have neglected your music for years," she began, "but I really need to retire and I want you to take over my studio. You would be perfect!

I will coach you for a time and will be there to support you."

The goose bumps and vibrations moving through my body at that moment were a sign that this was the calling I had been waiting for all my life. Life's choices had forced me to put my music on hold for eighteen years to get married and raise my family, and now I was being asked to give vocal lessons. I had never done this before! Could I do it?

I was being called back to my soul's purpose, to teach and perhaps even to perform.

I asked my then ex-husband what I should do.

He looked at me and said, "Do what you like. Why don't you continue studying and perform?" To this day he doesn't remember saying that, but the moment he did, tears began to run down my face and my soul opened up. I turned towards the window to hide my tears.

After he left I wondered, *Why am I crying? Why all these tears?* Today I realize it was my essence opening up, confirming what LOVE was instructing me to do.

I took over her studio and went back to university to finish my music degree.

I looked for and found a vocal/music teacher in Toronto, where I had studied many years ago. To my amazement my gift was still there!

Two years later, "Bravo! Encore!" filled the auditorium. I had received a standing ovation at my first concert!

I began the concert feeling blessed because a local tenor, renowned in our community, who had studied in New York had agreed to perform with me; what a privilege that had been. And to also have received a standing ovation! I thought I had died and gone to Heaven.

It didn't take long for the more experienced teachers and judges to begin taking note of the students coming from the north and wondering who their teacher was.

In two years, five of my students were accepted at the elite Glenn Gould School of Performance-something unheard of before. One is presently finishing his studies in Italy and is destined to please audiences all over the world. The others are continuing their vocal studies in performance.

The question What would LOVE do? had led and supported me.

I know LOVE gives everyone the gift of their soul, sends them the words they need to hear; it opens their heart's doors, but one must ask for it and allow it. The most painful, most beautiful, and empowering words I have ever heard were "I don't love you anymore."

LOVE ASKS ...

1. Did you ever lose the love of your life?

2. What became of you afterward?

3. Did you grow to see how the pain would be able to benefit you?

LOVE DELIVERS MY GRAND PIANO
~ LOVE's Gift To Me ~
Diana Holloway

The time had finally come. I had wanted a grand piano my entire life and after forty-five years of dreaming and thinking about it I decided I was going to do it! It was time! But how?

I didn't know much about grand pianos other than that they were expensive. I soon found out how expensive ... they could cost as much as fifteen thousand dollars!

I can't afford that! my logical mind kept thinking but my dream kept saying, *What would LOVE do?*

I knew LOVE was not a tease! LOVE wouldn't give me the desire for something and then not send me what I needed to get it. However, if I say I can't, I'm right ... I can't.

I kept hearing LOVE say, "Be patient. Wait." I decided to wait, but I began my research. I made my list, the type of wood and the make I wanted, second-hand and Canadian made. It had to have curled legs and be 5 feet and 2 inches in length and most importantly, it had to be affordable.

I also wanted the piano to be sold by someone who was divorced, and a lover of music. All that was left was to wait and wait, and that I did. That's not to say that every time I went to Toronto I didn't search the streets high and low making connections.

I also looked around my hometown of Sudbury, but to no avail.

It was nine months later that I got the phone call. Nine months! New birth. Interesting! "Diana, your piano is here."

The call didn't come from some long-lost music teacher, nor was it one of the connections I had made in Toronto. It was the wife of my current piano tuner.

She informed me that she hadn't purchased a grand piano with the intention of selling it in fifteen years, but she was certain this was the instrument I was looking for. She wanted me to go and see it ASAP because there were other people wanting it as well.

There it was! LOVE's gift to me. The exact colour, the exact size and the exact price. This was what I had been waiting for all my life! Exactly as I had imagined it.

This story isn't all pretty roses. LOVE's gift was also a final gift from my piano tuner's wife, who could have sold it to someone else at a higher price. She was soon diagnosed with cancer and died a year later.

I didn't receive it from someone who experienced a divorce; I received it from someone who experienced the final death of the body. Her physical self may no longer be with us but I know her spirit and LOVE smile upon me from up above knowing she had a hand in giving me a gift from LOVE, with LOVE.

LOVE ASKS ...

1. Do you believe desire is a good thing?

2. Have you been able to manifest the things you desire?

3. How do you feel when someone rejects you?

It is by going down into the abyss
that we recover the treasures of life.
Where you stumble,
there lies your treasure.

~Joseph Campbell ~
https://en.wikipedia.org/wiki/Joseph_Campbell

LOVE SENDS MY MASTER
~ I Am Worthy ~
Diana Holloway

"We need to find you a vocal teacher," my teacher said, "a master to continue your studies".

A vocal professor I knew from my past was the one I really wanted. I thought, *Ok LOVE, you returned me to my heart's passion and delivered my grand piano. It is time to provide me with a master if you want me to do your work. Send me the one that is in my best interest.*

During the annual Kiwanis festival, the adjudicator told me she knew an accompanist who was willing to have me audition. Once she heard me sing she would be able to recommend someone. I practiced and practiced and it all paid off, I sang like an angel for her.

"I know who would be perfect for you," she said, "I'll make the call."

She left without telling me who it could be. Later, I sat waiting for the audition. The moment I saw her amongst all the teachers I knew she was the one! I immediately recognized her as the teacher who I had auditioned for in exactly this same place, twenty years ago! It was perfect! She was the one!

"Yes," she said after listening to me, "tomorrow you may have a lesson."

My heart skipped for joy the entire way out, reliving the memory of the eleven-year-old.

When I arrived at my hotel a red carpet lay before me and large bedroom slippers greeted me, feeling symbolic of my future. Ah, I felt I had made it to the next level. This was my calling. This was my new career. Once again LOVE sent me what I needed when I needed it.

LOVE ASKS ...

1. Do you believe, when the student is ready, the teacher will appear?

2. Do you know that the teacher must also be ready for the student?

3. Who has been one of your most important teachers?

LOVE GOES HOME
~ Goodbye My Friend ~
Fern Rancourt

In 1995, I attended a two-weekend course on palliative care to learn how to be with people who were dying. Before I was fully qualified, I was asked to sit with an elderly lady who was alone and very sick in a nursing home. I didn't feel qualified but said I would do it after asking *What would LOVE do?* Little did I know that these were her final moments and that I would come back so transformed from these few hours spent by her side that I had to sit and write about it and dedicate it to her, the best palliative care teacher I had.

TO MY 90-YEAR-OLD FRIEND

When I was asked to go and accompany you
on your last journey, I felt inadequate and insecure.
After all, I had not yet completed my training
program as a palliative care volunteer.

But when the coordinators told me they felt I could
do it I hesitantly, but gladly, accepted.

So, I went empty handed and a little worried but full
of unconditional LOVE to be with you that night, not
knowing that it would be your last.

You appeared frail and uneasy yet you seemed
detached and peaceful as if you had transcended
all pain.

You had difficulty breathing; your eyes were half opened and distant as if you already perceived another reality.

Your right arm lay lifeless and cold on the warm bedcover. I gently stroked your hair and, as I was told, I delicately put my hand close to yours to let you know that you were not alone.

I felt very little talk was needed at this ultimate moment of your life. There are times where silence goes far beyond than words.

I tried reading a few pages of On Death and Dying but I had difficulty concentrating on the words dancing in front of my eyes in the dim light of that night.

The reality that I was involved in was so much more actual and vivid than the one that the book was conveying to me!

After moving a little uncomfortably once in a while for about an hour, you finally fell asleep seemingly relieved.
I looked at you for a long time sending you thoughts of Light and LOVE and wondering what was going on deep within you.

Then after a short time your breathing started to change.

I think that you imperceptibly let go of every attachment you still had and silently prepared yourself for your final and most important journey.

As if she knew you were dying a nurse came at that precise moment and, without a word, both of us sacredly witnessed your last breath ...

I thought, mystified, so this is what it is to die!

You just slowly cease to breathe and you enter into another dimension, invisible but no less real.

To my surprise, I was not afraid. On the contrary, I felt very humbled and privileged to have been asked to come and enter this sacred place of yours.

Quietly, I left your silent room and still by the simplicity of your death, I came back home rehearsing in my mind this last hour and a half with you.

I was a changed person.
When I first met you in that lonely, semi-dark room, you were a complete stranger.

But in a very short time you seemed to have become like a grandmother figure, someone I have always known.
I could imagine you crossing this last threshold and being met by the One we call God.

I believe that at the hour of our death we clearly understand the mystery of life that goes on eternally and we become embraced by the Light!

Thank you, my dear friend, for having taught me so much in so little time!
I will always remember these precious moments I spent with you on this unique night of your going home!

Thank you Fern for sharing such an intimate moment with the rest of the world.

LOVE ASKS ...

1. Have you been present when a soul was leaving its body?

2. What did it feel like? Sound like? Look like?

3. Does being with a person who is dying frighten you?

HOW CAN I SERVE NOW?

Do you want to know?

Do you want to be a part of it?

Where two or more are gathered

In My name

~ IN LOVE ~

There I AM!

*A thousand words
will not leave so deep an impression
as one deed.*

~ Henrik Ibsen ~
https://www.biography.com/people/henrik-ibsen-37014

LOVE GETS NOMINATED
~ All Part of the Big Picture ~

"It's election night, I wonder how many will show up?" I was thinking out loud as I was getting ready to go to my monthly Business and Professional Women's (BPW) Club meeting.

"Are you running for anything?" John asked.

"I haven't volunteered for anything but I know I will come home with something," I replied.

"Are they going to make you president?" he continued, a bit concerned.

"Are you crazy! Why would they do that? I've only been in the club a short while and don't know enough for that position. I'll probably get the chair of fundraising because I collected a lot of door prizes for our Speaker Night," I replied. "Nothing more."

"We'll see," he half-whispered as I walked out the door.

As expected, attendance was low but enough proxies had been received to have quorum, so elections could proceed after dinner. I chatted with a young woman who was Provincial President of a Union. I was impressed that one so young, especially a woman, was given such a responsible position. We hit it off quickly because we spoke the same spiritual language.

When I asked how she became president she said, "I was nominated and thought I wouldn't get in because I was so new and young and didn't really have any experience but I told God, if you want me to do this I am yours."

She continued, "I'm often given tasks I don't know anything about and keep saying 'Send me what I need,' and I always get it."

"I know," I added excitedly. "Isn't it amazing how it always works out so perfectly? I do exactly the same thing."

We continued exchanging stories, delighting in each other's trust and joy of service.

"May I interrupt you?" another member asked a few minutes later.

"Sure, what's up?" I asked.

"I was recently talking to Shirley MacLaine and she tells me I have to get some help," she said.

"The actress Shirley MacLaine?" I asked as shivers ran up my spine.

"Where? When did you see her?"

"In Toronto a couple of months ago when I was auditioning for Tom Cruise's new movie, Dream Spell."

"What part does Shirley have?" I asked.

"She doesn't. She is acting as Tom's spiritual and energy advisor," our budding actress added.

"She told me I have the part but that I have to prepare for it. She asked where I lived and when I told her Sudbury she asked, 'Why?'

"I told her it was because I liked the bush. She then said that that was ok, I could travel to do my work. Shirley then told me I had to find a spiritual advisor in Sudbury, one with the initials C. M. You are the only spiritual advisor I know and your initials are C.M. Would you help me?" she pleaded.

"Glad to," I replied. "I guess the future is getting closer."

'What do you mean?" she asked.

"Twelve years ago, I attended Shirley's workshop on Chakras in New York. I was one of about twelve hundred people and when she invited those who were interested in working in the center she was planning, to write their names in the book at the back of the room, about eleven hundred people rushed to do so while I stayed put.

"A little voice told me 'Don't bother. You'll be working with her in the future.' The same little voice I heard in Holland while I was reading her book Out On A Limb that said, "You are going to meet Shirley MacLaine."

"I thought, *Yeah right! We're both redheads, we both tap dance, I'll just knock on her door and say, 'Hey Shirl, let's do lunch.'* Three years later I met her at her workshop and spoke to her for about two minutes.

"She probably wouldn't remember me however, that voice said we would be working together in the future … guess the future is getting closer. I'd LOVE to help get you ready for your part. Give me a call when it's time."

The BPW dinner meetings were sometimes a little dry. This one was anything but! I was already having a fantastic night! Then a much-respected member of the club began asking me questions about my work, which always gives me a natural buzz. I was flying high and nothing was going to ground me, not even elections. It was time to get down to business.

The president made an unexpected announcement, stating she was stepping down and the vice president would not be able to replace her because she had just received a work promotion that made her unavailable. The first thing that had to be done was elect a new president.

The much-respected member who had been asking me about my work immediately nominated me and the president of the union seconded the motion. I was in shock! When asked if I would let my name stand I asked for a moment to decide, quickly went within and asked, *What would LOVE do?* and saw a big *YES* in my head.

"Yes," I replied, praying to God someone else would be nominated.

Another member who had ten years in the club and had held many committee positions was also nominated.

When we were asked to speak I concluded my very short presentation with the words I had shared the month before when I was their guest speaker,

"Ladies you will always make the right decision when you ask your heart, *What would LOVE do?* and vote for whomever your heart names. That person will be the one this club needs at this time."

I closed, all the while praying that I was not the one. The next thing I heard after the secret ballots were counted, "Welcome your new president, Caroline McIntosh." I almost passed out!

I thought I had joined for socializing and networking! John must be psychic!

Three weeks later I was at a provincial conference, voting on resolutions regarding sex slavery, the morning-after pill, homelessness, the employment standards act and more! What had I gotten myself into?

I quickly learned the Business and Professional Women's Club was on five continents, in over one hundred countries, had representation at the United Nations, and that my club was the largest in Canada. A few months later, five minutes before I was to leave for Michigan to graduate from the World Service Order, I received a phone call from our Member of Parliament inviting me to participate at a roundtable discussion with the Federal Finance Minister, Mr. Martin. Each participant was to be allowed five minutes to discuss the economy of our city.

What do I know about such matters? I make a little money and spend a lot! Panic again! I called upon the BPW's past national and local president and asked her to gather information I could use.

The meeting was to be held and covered by the media on Tuesday evening, and I was returning home that morning! I wouldn't have much time to prepare my presentation.

I did my best and apparently it was well received. At that time, it was rumored that this man could be the next leader of our country.

LOVE knows where LOVE needs to be and it didn't take me too long to start putting the pieces together, it was all part of the bigger picture!

My teacher and spiritual advisor, Tom Sawyer, had told me one year prior, that the politicians and businesses would support the not for profit club I was establishing because we would be helping them do their work. Here I was, suddenly and unexpectedly placed right in the middle of both.

The cosmic giggle kicks in every time I witness how all the pieces and people come together at the perfect moment in the perfect way.

I just remembered another piece of the puzzle. Several years ago, I began hosting an annual Psychic Pyjama Party, and at the last one the participants had asked me to do a reading for each of them and I agreed to do so if they did one for me in return.

My dear friend Louise was the last to speak, "It's strange but I see you taking a detour in about five to six months."

"Does it have anything to do with the club I want to start up?" I asked, not wanting to hear anything that would be against it.

"Not directly," she replied, "I see you on a conveyor belt with a torch held high in your right hand and people following you. That's all I am getting."

Exactly five and one-half months later I became president of the BPW. That was the big detour; all the training for my club was put on hold. One year later I asked Louise to get back on that conveyor belt with me and answer some more questions. "How long is this belt moving?" I asked.

"Two years," she replied.

"How is it affecting my club?" I continued.

"I see little groups gathering everywhere and at the end of two years you step off the conveyor belt, flick on a switch and everything is in place to take off!"

Great news. My term as BPW president lasts two years. It will be time for my club to have its birthday party and be introduced to the world.

Was LOVE using John to prepare me for the future? Maybe I should listen more carefully when he speaks.

LOVE ASKS ...

1. Have you ever been asked to do something you did not feel qualified to do?

2. Did you accept the challenge?

3. What did you gain or learn as a result of being pushed beyond your comfort level?

LOVE'S CLUB
~ Uniting and Empowering ~

Since retiring from the military in 1981, I have been leading workshops for groups, businesses, schools (from kindergarten to university), on energy, stress management, healing, spirituality, discovering one's life's purpose, death, bullying, suicide and more. I have also worked with the elderly, who would not leave their homes for fear of being mugged, or who were experiencing depression because they had no one to share their lives, wisdom, and laughter with. I have also helped families deal with grief due to death by suicide, murder, illness, and natural causes.

Whenever I've shared my knowledge and tools I have repeatedly heard, "Why isn't this taught in school? Isn't there some place we can go to learn these things, a club or something?"

If I hear something three times that is a sign for me to do it. Well, three hundred times later the need is finally being met. A prototype for future use in personal, family, community, and global lives dreamed over a two-year period is now ready to be introduced to the world.

I knew it would have to have a special name. One militia group I was working with said. "Let's call ourselves Spiritual Warriors."

That didn't feel right. Many names were suggested and when I thought we had it I would ask, what would LOVE call it?

I was always told, "You will know it when you hear it. You won't even have to check it out."

It came watching the Oprah show! Oprah was so excited with the buckets of money coming in for her Angel Network she grabbed a guest by the arm and said, Isn't it wonderful! We're all members of 'the God Squad!'

That was it! I loved the sound of it, but not the feel. I knew people would hear God and think church, religion, yours vs. mine, and that separates people.

Our club was about unity so I went back to LOVE and asked for help and got it. It was so simple ...

The G.O.D. S.Q.U.A.D. (G.S.)
stood for
Goodness Opening Doors ...
Spiritually Quietly Unafraid Aware Delightfully.

We became
The G.O.D. S.Q.U.A.D. Serving Communities, Inc.
A Not for Profit Club for Everyone from Schoolyard
to Graveyard

MISSION STATEMENT - To unite and empower people to better LOVE themselves, so they in turn, can better LOVE and serve the rest of humanity and the planet.

MOTTO - What Would LOVE Do? Sound familiar?

TEACHERS/LEADERS - Many people of all ages are willing to share their life's experiences; they want to matter, to make a difference.

Those people are easy to find. Twelve teachers between the ages of twelve and seventy-five are presently being trained.

MEMBERSHIP - Is open to everyone from schoolyard to graveyard, especially those considered society's rejects.

MEMBERSHIP FEE - $30 worth of good deeds to be paid annually. At first it was a concern because the poor and homeless don't have the money. Community sponsoring is ideal but not always feasible for those who want to but can't afford to for various reasons. I fretted over this until I finally asked *What would LOVE do?* and was told, "Trust, everything you need will come. Have each member earn their fee. No one is to pay his or her own way in. Everyone must enter as equals. You will have benefactors."

LOVE is always so simple. If trusting were only that easy. To include everyone and offend no one, sponsors would not be required to pay anyone.

They would simply provide opportunities for applicants to do good deeds and sign a sponsor sheet verifying the deed was done and its value. In this way, anyone could be both a sponsor and a member.

MEMBERSHIP FEE $100 - Applicants confident enough may assist the club raise some money and earn credits towards their Fundraising Badge by approaching businesses or individuals to provide $100 worth of good deeds.

The sponsor will pay the $100 directly to the G.O.D. S.Q.U.A.D.

BASIC TRAINING - All identified with a name tag that reads: Caroline ... I'm I.T.   (I.T. = In Training)

MEMBERS WILL LEARN THE FOLLOWING IN THE FIVE BRANCHES

- Spiritually - The Light Affirmation, how to re-connect with one's Spiritual Self, how everything they do affects the whole
- Quietly - Introduction to Meditation, Psychic Self-Defense, (Protect self from others' negativity)
- Unafraid - CPR, Basic First Aid and Self-Defense
- Aware - Basic ESP Training (Extra Sensory Perception to develop intuition)
- Delightfully - Clown Course, Dolphin Course

When possible and appropriate, members will learn what they want when they want, with others of all ages - as has been done for the last sixty-five years in an ashram in India. Being educated in this fashion enables everyone to learn teamwork, leadership, listening, cooperation, patience. It made the students in the Indian ashram better qualified to enter higher education institutions than their counterparts attending traditional schools.

Once Membership Dues and Basic Training are completed, the applicant must then create a Personal Pledge that will be repeated as his/her Oath to LOVE which will be lived for the rest of his/her life.

Once pledged, the applicant becomes a full member of the club, and is invited to attend classes.

All graduates of basic training are now called Manifestors and can begin training to specialize in their field of interest.

Classes dealing with stress, fears, anger, grief, guilt, self-esteem, nature, survival, dreams, death, social and environmental issues, and so forth, conducted by community volunteers will be offered.

Members' needs and interests will determine the subjects taught.

ALL CLASSES INCLUDE ...

- Meditation
- Questions - Relating to last class
- Teaching - Volunteer teaches something of interest to members.
- Exercise - Related to Teaching. All lesson must be applicable to life.
- Sharing - All get opportunity to share their experience in exercise.
- Healing - All give and receive hands on healing
- Discipline - Determined by teacher, all members practice till next class.
- Socializing - Coffee, chatting, etc.
- Farewell - Instead of Goodbye we say, "Go to your destiny."

SOME AWARDS THAT MAY BE EARNED ...

- Spiritually - Healing, Dreams, Rescue Work, Crystals, Animal Totems, Power, Symbols, Sex, Religion
- Quietly – Self-Discipline, Service, Finance, Health, Mental Diet, Tai Chi, Photography, Computers
- Unafraid - Public Speaking, Survival Skills, Fears, Combat Sports, Braille, Signing, Driving, Courage, Volunteerism
- Aware - Interspecies Communication, Special Needs, Gardening, Cooking, Craft/Trade, Environment, Social Graces, Business Etiquette
- Delightfully - Games, Theatre, Music, Arts and Crafts, Organization, Animal Care, Woodworking, Taxidermy

SEVEN LEVELS OF AWARDS IN ALL FIVE BRANCHES ...

1) Basic/Introduction
2) Serving Self
3) Serving Community
4) Serving Spirit
5) Mentoring Student
6) Student Mentors
7) Business/Global

Example: In the Delightful Branch if a member wants to learn Woodworking, a carpenter in the community will volunteer to teach.

1) Safety, handling, and care of tools, and blueprint/pattern reading
2) Member makes something for self like a little bench
3) Member makes something for the community, for sale

4) Member makes something totally original, including pattern

5) Member mentors a student, teaching safety, handling, care of tools, and so forth

6) Member's Student becomes a mentor

7) Member learns basics in setting up his/her own business as in a hobby shop or serves globally as in Housing for Humanity.

SPECIAL PROJECTS ...

The club's Special Projects will include fun activities that will help in fundraising while allowing members to serve their community.

As you can see, it is quite a project and I know it has the potential to become global. Every time I hear of a child going into school with a gun to kill in anger, of mass suicides, of seniors hidden and abused in their homes, of Native children sniffing gasoline, or disgruntled former employees firing guns, snipers, terrorists and the rest of the pain and fear on the planet I know Goodness Opening Doors can make a big difference.

If you are reading this book but have no interest in joining the G.S. you still can serve LOVE.

How?

If your neighbor hasn't been seen out and about for a while ...
What would LOVE do?

If you hear neighbours screaming and fighting ...
What would LOVE do?

If youth in your community are getting in trouble ...
What would LOVE do?

If a friend is in the hospital ...
What would LOVE do?

If there were an earthquake, flood, plane crash ...
What would LOVE do?

If you win a lottery and wish to share it ...
What would LOVE do?

If, if, if, is such a small word yet it carries so much weight and guilt ... if only we had known.

LOVE does know and wants to help and serve us as we help and serve It. It always knows what is best for all concerned at all times.

I know the G.O.D. S.Q.U.A.D will take off; it will have what is needed to do so.

It is the reason this book was written. I was looking for a way to market the G.O.D. S.Q.U.A.D. and my brilliant mentor suggested I needed an umbrella/roof that all my projects could come under.

MY BUSINESS –

LOVE'S OPEN HOUSE ~ LOH
Your H.O.M.E. Away From HOME
(Heaven On Mother Earth)
Come to LOH to get HIGH on LIFE!

LOH IS HOME of The G.O.D. S.Q.U.A.D. Serving Communities, Inc.

LOH OFFERS - Services, Products and Special Events, that bring Spirituality into All Aspects of Life for All Ages.

Services - Motivational Speakers, Healings, Psychic Readings, Workshops, Classes, The Natural Process™, Spiritual Ceremonies, Fundraising

Products - CDs, DVDs, Books, eBooks, EClasses, Ezines, Dog Tags, Teleclasses, T-Shirts

Special Events -

- ♥ AWAKENINGS … Movies that reach into your heart and turn your light on. Hosted to date … Indigo, Indigo Evolution, The Secret, Illusions, Conversations With God, Peaceful Warrior, Celestine Prophecy, Star Dreams, 2012 Space Odyssey
- ♥ INTENSIVE METAPHYSICAL RETREATS - AKA – Weekend Psychic Pyjama Parties
- ♥ LOVE'S MIRACLES *n MESSAGES - Inspirational Speaking and Healing from the platform.
- ♥ M.A.F.Y. - Mastermind Awakenings For Youth

LET'S PARTNER

The G.O.D. S.Q.U.A.D and LOVE'S OPEN HOUSE want to partner with Youth, Seniors, Churches, Schools, Businesses, Politicians, First Nations, Homeless, Special Needs, Environmentalists, AND YOU!

My wish is to bring the dream world down into the real world; to make the invisible visible; to do what is spoken of in the well-known Lord's Prayer, "Thy will be done on Earth as it is in Heaven."

Certainly takes on a new meaning doesn't it?

LOVE ASKS ...

1. Would YOU be interested in getting involved with The G.O.D. S.Q.U.A.D.?

2. What would you do if you felt a neighbour was being abused?

3. Would you like to see a G.O.D. S.Q.U.A.D Serving YOUR Community?

LOVE'S INVITATION

~ You Make A Difference ~

LOVE invites you, dear reader, to be its partner, co-creator.

LOVE invites you to connect hearts in grocery stores, in schools, on the freeways, in hospitals, prisons, courthouses, your home, everywhere.

LOVE invites you to be in the hearts of your children, spouses, partners, friends, enemies, religious and political leaders, teachers, parents, police, prisoners, counselors, the rich the poor, the ignorant and gifted-everyone.

LOVE invites you to LOVE and serve each other and everything that lives on this planet.

LOVE invites you to be your true self, to be LOVE in action.

LOVE, the Light, the life force in every atom of energy, is all, knows all, and LOVEs all equally!

Every time you choose LOVE over hate, anger, fear, revenge, jealousy, greed, lust, addictions, sadness, suicide, and everything that causes pain and separation, you are making a difference, you matter.

Every time you think or do anything, you are influencing me and everyone else, because LOVE inside my cells registers what you have done. I may not know it at the conscious level, but at the subconscious and super conscious level I do.

LOVE inside you allows you choices; allows you to influence the whole in a positive or negative way.

Are your thoughts and actions making others weak or strong?

Do you begin to understand mob mentality?

LOVE inside a mother's cells registers everything her child does. Do you begin to understand how she knows her child is hurt or in trouble thousands of miles away?

It is physically impossible to feel pain, fear, and anger in the presence of LOVE!

Remember the feeling of being 'in LOVE.' Yesterday's problems no longer bother you. You feel like you could conquer the world.

Why?

Because ...LOVE changes your brain chemistry. The brain begins to produce endorphins, nature's drug, pain reliever. It gives you a natural 'high.' Do you now understand how those being tortured can die with a look of bliss on their faces?

Medicine is beginning to truly understand LOVE's power. That's why a loving family and friends are so important in the healing process.

Do you understand why nature and animals (the non–judgmental faces of LOVE) nurture us, especially when living in stressful areas such as hospitals, prisons, seniors' residences, and other places like the concrete jungles of the cities?

LOVE is the 'Krazy Glue' of the universe! It holds everything together. Nothing can exist without it.

A fun way to explain it to children is to use play dough and ask them to pretend to be God ... creating, shaping trees, stars, animals, rocks, little boys and girls, using the play dough as the foundation, the raw material for everything. They then paint, cover, and dress their creations differently and in the end, everything looks different.

However ... remove all the outside coverings, get down to the source of all that is, and you will find that every single atom is made of the same play dough, that IS all, KNOWS all ... LOVE. Each and every one of us looks different because LOVE likes variety and wants us to master loving everyone and everything equally.

LOVE is not a tease. It will not give your heart a passionate dream and not send everything needed to make it come true. You just have breathe and be willing for it to come through you by saying, "Send me what I need, I will do it."

Remember, "Ask and ye shall receive"? It's time to move your dreams from the invisible world down to this physical world because LOVE wants you to share your dream, Its dream, with everyone.

LOVE cannot be divided, conquered, or lost. We have all seen videos of a sperm connecting with an egg to create a cell. Then the cell splits in half, destined to become a fetus. Did it become divided, conquered, or lost?

Yes, it divided, however it did not become two halves ... it became two wholes! Think of it! The more you give of your LOVE, the more you split it, the more you create.

'What goes around comes around', multiplied! Returns to you ... just like echoes!

LOVE lost is never truly lost. It may appear to feel that way when you are letting your human self take over. Yes, we are supposed to feel and experience human loss, grief, anger and so on, because we came to Earth to experience feelings, however, we are not supposed to live in it forever. We are to experience it, feel is and see IF we can remember who we truly are, invincible, infinite divine beings of light!

Remember that truth. You are a magnificent being of LOVE having a human experience and as soon as you reconnect to your loving self your human self experiences peace, harmony, wholeness. LOVE is the greatest power. LOVE is the only power.

LOVE is very efficient. It does not waste one atom of energy to get a job done.

How much energy does it take to have power thru force? Blackmail, intimidation, torturing, threatening, hitting, yelling and so forth, all require a great deal of energy.

How much energy does it take to have power through LOVE? Nada! 0! Zero! Nul! Nothing! You don't even have to say a word ... not even think ... just sit and Be LOVE.

If you are filled with LOVE and your friend wants to buy you something for your birthday, LOVE inside that person knows everything about you and will give your friend the thought to buy the perfect gift you have been wanting yet haven't said a thing about!

You can have all the power in the world without doing a single thing other than being LOVE!

The quickest way to get rid of an enemy is to make him or her your friend. Have you seen the movie Ben Hur? If not, rent the video.

Witness true LOVE in action and its power when the slave Ben Hur is not allowed to have a drink of water when everyone else is. A man appears (you never see His face throughout the movie, you know it is Jesus) and he fills a ladle with water and gives it to Ben Hur. A centurion begins to yell and raises his whip to strike Jesus until he looks into His eyes (just thinking of this scene moves me to tears).

You see the centurion's anger (How dare you challenge my authority type of look) become confusion, (Why are you not afraid of me?) fear (What power do you have), submission, shame, LOVE, and awe (You LOVE me! How can you LOVE someone so ugly? You LOVE me?!!)

All without Jesus saying one word.

Do you remember being really nasty to someone and that person chose to LOVE you knowing what you had done? Looking into that person's eyes became very difficult. You felt dirty, ugly, unworthy.

You thought, *You still LOVE me? How can you LOVE someone so ugly, so dirty? I am so unworthy!*

LOVE continues to lovingly touch you until you are ready to remember and LOVE yourself.

The person you wanted to hurt is now someone you would die for. You can't believe someone would still LOVE someone so ugly, so dirty, so unworthy!" That is the power of LOVE.

When you let go of the LOVE of power, you will have the power of LOVE!

LOVE is what we are here to be, to demonstrate. One simple way to do that is with the LOVE'S MAGICAL CONNECTION ... the pink ribbon story.

You, dear reader, are invited to create Magical Connections with anyone, everyone, especially with those who have hurt you. The only thing you must always remember is to ask for permission first.

If you have any doubt the person wants it simply let the ribbon float down to the person's feet and forget about it. It will be picked up at the perfect moment.

The person you are creating a Magical Connection with, at that moment, may begin to think about you and begin to feel warm and fuzzy inside. LOVE may move you to share your story with the rest of the world. If so, send it to me. It may be the perfect one to inspire and empower someone else to do the same and even more.

One very important thing you are asked to remember about LOVE, no matter what you choose to think, say, or do, you are loved exactly as you are, EVERY SINGLE MOMENT! Never forget that!

LOVE ASKS ...

1. Did you know LOVE cannot be divided, conquered or lost?

2. Are you willing to try to make your enemy your friend?

3. Have you ever been loved by a person you were nasty to?

Ladies there are bigger goals in life than being a good woman to a man.
Be a good woman to yourself.

~ Farrah Gray ~
https://www.visualcv.com/farrahgray

LOVE'S CLOSING
~ Sufi Chant ~

How should I end my classes, workshops, meetings and gatherings? I wondered.

I knew I wanted something special, something that would leave a positive impression and be memorable. When I asked *What would LOVE do?* I flashed back to the workshop I attended in New York City conducted by a Reiki Master teacher. She led our group of fifty or more Reiki Masters through one exercise that changed many lives that day.

"I want everyone in a circle walking in a clockwise direction," she began, "and while doing so I want you to imagine your parents in the center of the circle. You are going to sing the Sufi Chant to them," she instructed.

I had never heard the Sufi Chant before but that one-line chant left a lump in my throat when I thought of my parents hearing, *All I ask of you is forever to remember me as loving you.*

We continued walking and singing the Sufi Chant to our parents until we heard, "Change direction and place someone who has hurt you in the center and sing the Sufi Chant to that person."

Singing, *All I ask of you is forever to remember me as loving you*, was NOT what I wanted to say to that so and so, but the words worked their magic on me.

I began to soften and actually began to mean them. We changed direction and sang it to someone we had hurt. That was more painful than when someone had hurt me.

The guilt and shame surfaced. Once again, I softened and began to feel the power of LOVE's healing words.

We continued changing directions and placing different people, groups, and situations in the center: our birth, death, bosses, teachers, political and religious leaders, mother earth and so on.

There were four opera singers in the group, so their voices added to the impact that was experienced by everyone. We were finally invited to sit down and relax. I must have gone through two boxes of tissues in that short period of time.

"How long do you think you have been walking and singing the Sufi Chant?"

Usually a good judge of time when in an altered state, I mumbled, "About twenty minutes."

"One hour and a half!" she said smilingly, knowing we would be surprised. No wonder I was bushed, totally drained, yet so uplifted! Well, that would certainly be a powerful way to bring closure to any gathering, I thought. *I wonder if it will have the same impact.*

It didn't take me long to find out. That weekend I had a children's workshop and timed the closure so the parents could join us.

I bowed and sang the chant to each child and parent and then proceeded to lead them through an experience similar to my first one in New York.

It was so powerful I had to spend some time with a parent who broke down crying because of the pain that had surfaced that was ready to be healed.

From that moment on, it became a tradition. Regardless of the occasion, whether it was a spiritual, educational, political, business or social gathering, everyone got to hear and participate in it. LOVE always geared it to the needs of the group, ensuring it was always appropriate. Children especially, LOVE hearing it as they go to sleep.

Your Creator and I Sing to You

All I Ask of You Is Forever
To Remember Me As Loving You!

LISTEN TO SONG HERE
http://www.iamcaroline.com/

SING THE SUFI CHANT TO

- ♥ loved ones, alive or deceased
- ♥ Your pets and plants
- ♥ Your boss
- ♥ Your employees
- ♥ Some you've hurt
- ♥ Someone who's hurt you
- ♥ Politicians … Religious Leaders … Businesses
- ♥ Mother Earth and all who live on her
- ♥ To all and everyone

LOVE ASKS ...

1. Would you be willing to sing the Sufi chant to someone who hurt you?

2. Can you imagine someone you hurt singing it to you?

3. Would you consider singing it to those who have hurt you?

LOVE SAYS GOOD-BYE TO MRS. D.
~ The Perfection of Dying So Young ~

They were the school's rebels, special needs, society's rejects, and Mrs. D. was the only one who could get them to pay attention in class.

"Today is Friday and Friday means Fun Day," she told the children. No books were allowed unless they involved fun things like cooking, catalogues for shopping, and the like. The children Loved Mrs. D. as much as she Loved them, until she disappeared!

The supply teachers that replaced her immediately canceled Friday Fun Days. The children were told Mrs. D. was not returning because they were too bad. Needless to say, no teacher lasted more than one week, until Mary Theresa was sent to the school.

She immediately told them, "Mrs. D. is not returning because she has cancer and she is dying. It is not your fault." Miss. M., as she was called, continued, "We are going to do something very special for Mrs. D. I am going to put a desk and chair in the hall and if you want to talk to Mrs. D. you may take the tape recorder with you and sit in the chair and tell her a story, a joke, read a poem, say whatever you want.

"We will begin each day with a new tape and the Sufi Chant. At the end of the day we will close with the Sufi Chant and one of you will deliver it to her home so she can hear it because she misses you so much."

Each day a new tape was filled with all the LOVE those big hearts in little bodies could give. Each day it was delivered to Mrs. D.

One Monday evening Miss. M. was in my class and shared her experience with us. "You won't believe what happened in class today," she began.

"Johnny is the school's biggest bully. He sits at the back of the class and is known for being the troublemaker. We have been doing Mrs. D.'s tapes for one week now but I didn't know what an impact it was having on the students until Johnny started acting up in class."

"What happened?" we asked, quite concerned.

"He started making sounds at his desk and looked like he was up to something. I decided to casually stroll by to see what he was doing.

"As I approached, it became quite clear that he was humming the Sufi Chant to himself and upon closer inspection I noticed he was drawing a picture of Mrs. D. with the chant written on it.

Before I knew it the whole class was quietly humming the Sufi Chant. I have never felt so in awe of anyone before as I was with Johnny. Thank you for teaching me that chant."

"Thank you for passing it on and for being an inspiration to those children," I replied.

Mrs. D. passed away a few months later.

Every room in the funeral home was overflowing with people of all ages who had been touched by her LOVE and compassion. I sat next to a woman in her eighties who said, "Isn't it sad one should die so young?"

She was shocked when I replied, "Isn't it perfect that she should die so young?"

"What do you mean?" she asked angrily.

"How many people would be here today if Mrs. D. had died in her eighties or nineties?" I asked.

"Not too many," her elderly friend replied. I then told her the story of Mrs. D.'s students and how her death provided LOVE an opportunity to let her know how much she was loved.

It provided her students the opportunity to share their LOVE and to learn the Sufi Chant. None of that would have happened if Mrs. D. had not died at fifty-two years of age.

I also shared my belief that when we have completed our earthly work, our souls will always choose to go 'home' in a way that will serve as many people as possible, like Mrs. D.

"I guess you're right," she replied. "I never would have thought of it that way."

The Sufi Chant was sung at her funeral by everyone who gathered to say farewell and thank you. Three years later I found out that the Sufi Chant was inscribed on Mrs. D.'s headstone.

You never know the impact you have on another's life.

I am passing it on to you so you can use it to make a difference.

Always remember your Creator saying ...

All I ask of you
Is Forever
To Remember Me As Loving You!

LOVE ASKS ...

1. Do you know someone like Mrs. D?

2. Do you believe we choose to die in a way that will serve as many people as possible?

3. Do you see how rebels can change when they are loved?

AUTHOR
CAROLINE McINTOSH, Rev.
hts Satnam

Caroline is a gifted and energized spirit, dedicated to inspiring others to soar to greater heights. Since childhood she has moved between the worlds of a mystic and that of a clown, allowing Spirit to use her in whatever way is necessary to turn on someone's light.

Since leaving the military in 1981, Caroline followed her heart's desires swimming with dolphins, meditating and studying with saints and psychics in India, Russia, Hawaii, Tibet, Egypt, Britain and the USA; meeting Shirley MacLaine (as Spirit said she would) and other famous teachers and healers worldwide; getting ordained in the Order Of Melchizedec; walking on fire, lecturing, painting, writing, doing TV specials; conducting intensive workshops for all ages (specializing in suicide and bullying).

She certified in and practiced Psychic/Spiritual Healing, Reflexology, Therapeutic Touch, Dream Analysis, Mariel Healing, Mediumship and Advanced Integrated Awareness Techniques. Caroline is a Reiki Master, a member of the World Service Order and is ordained in the non-denominational Order of Melchizedec.

As president of the largest Business and Professional Women's Club in Canada she has conducted presentations on, *Business and Spirituality ...The Dynamic Duel/Duo* showing businesses how to align the two to move from success to significance.

Her glimpse of the future revealed the G.O.D. S.Q.U.A.D. Serving Communities, Inc. could unit and empower people on a global level.

She brings a unique perspective to self-fulfillment and success, openly sharing insights from her former military life and personal spiritual journey of self-discovery and reconnection to 'Home.'

She encourages others to explore and expand their horizons, and to seek simplicity and harmony in daily living by asking The Magical Question ... What Would LOVE Do?

As she stood in front of the audience at one of her first presentations she heard, "Be still and do not speak until you feel our presence and when you do, speak softly, slowly and enunciate every word."

She did as she was told. She stood, waited and a vision of Jesus at the top of the hill surrounded by the multitude filled her with LOVE as tears flowed down her cheeks.

"If you could see what I am seeing now," she whispered as she slowly opened her eyes. There wasn't a dry eye in the house. That was just the beginning.

She continues to share LOVE's message with all who care to listen. She currently lives in Northern Ontario doing presentations in schools, workshops,

inspirational speaking and healings. She is begun to travel again after a long absence due to the death of her parents and other experiences, life sent her way.

One never knows what she may be doing next, only that it is Spirit and Joy inspired.

Caroline is available as a speaker, workshop leader and for personal consultations. She invites you to contact her to ask what *hts* Satnam means.

*Blessed are those who
can give without remembering
and take without forgetting.*

~ Elizabeth Bibesco ~
https://www.poemhunter.com/elizabeth-bibesco/biography/

CONTRIBUTORS

Jean Lafleur

Born in 1928 - deceased 2016, this mother of seven, grandmother of twelve and great-grandmother of nine recently retired as a psychic/healer to devote her time to her childhood dream-to write, and write she did. Spirit kept inspiring her with so many stories, poems and songs she often worked on as many as five at a time. Some of her most popular are ...

HEAVEN'S FOR GIVING ~ Blessings NOT Punishment. Case studies of Jean's clients who were healed. The stories trigger similar healings in the readers.

KEVIN & ASKEM ~ An Awesome Twosome. The story of a psychic dog, named after Jean's beloved Ask Him who died at 21, and his young master solving mysteries, bringing families together. It has the potential to become a Walt Disney Classic.

KEVIN & ASKEM ~ A Beaver Tale. A little booklet outlining the adventures of these two explorers and their discovery of beavers.

KEVIN & ASKEM ~ Deer Oh Dear! Will be the next in a series of adventures with different animals.

ANGELS IN DISGUISE ~ See With Your Heart NOT With Your Eyes ... A semi-autobiographical story of the angels in disguise that came into Jean's life revealing ways to find out if you've had some too. Jean earned her Angel Wings on 4 Nov 2016

Diana Holloway

Diana teaches vocal and music classes at Huntington University in Sudbury, Ontario and is renowned as a teacher who has produced students acclaimed at the international level. She performs at fundraising events and continues to promote young talent.

She is on a board of directors creating a mini senior's concert. Diana, a mother of two grown sons, lives in Sudbury and works full time in advertising.

Diana may be contacted by writing:

DIANA HOLLOWAY
465 Winchester, Sudbury, Ontario, Canada P3E 3T7

Email
Diana@northernlife.ca

Fern Rancourt

Fern, a senior French-Canadian woman who, in spite of multiple sclerosis, has always managed to fend for herself. For five years she produced acrylic paintings that were so realistic it seemed one could simply step into the scene.

An eternal spiritual searcher, Fern likes to learn about life and LOVE and excels in networking like-minded spirits. She has also excelled as a single parent raising two talented, amazing, children who have blossomed into bright, strong, spirits sharing their gifts with the world. Fern is presently lives in beautiful British Columbia, Canada.

DO YOU WANT MORE?

It's all up to you.

Do you want to read more or to submit your own story?

What Would LOVE Do?

For self, kids, pets, teens, parents, artists, nurses, doctors, military, teachers, lawyers, laborers, politicians, the earth, the dying, pet lovers, care givers, business owners, religious leaders, physically, mentally, emotionally challenged, and others?

Submit your stories and make it happen.

To help you, a story guideline will be available by

EMAIL

WhatWouldLoveDo@eastlink.ca

OR

Love@IAmCaroline.com

I have a habit of letting
my imagination run away from me.
It always comes back though ...
drenched with possibilities.

~ Valaida Fullwood ~
https://www.biblio.com/valaida-fullwood/author/2200292

TESTIMONIES

*Asking, "What would LOVE do?" can change you
into something more than what you presently are.
Because of Caroline, I found my chance and the way to
do that. For that I am profoundly grateful.*

~ John Reid, St. Catherine's, Ontario, Canada ~

*I met Caroline, not knowing why or how my life
would change ... man did it ever change!
By being her caring self, she opened my eyes to a world I
thought I knew. Her free sessions at the Women's
Centre proved she doesn't do it for money, it comes from
her heart! She taught LOVE is very powerful and it
starts by loving ourselves. Thank you. Thank you.
In French- Merci or mer sea, ha ha.
She also helped us laugh a lot.*

~ Anita Paquette, Drummondville, Quebec, Canada ~

*In 1989, when the family was undergoing a great deal
of stress, I began suffering from a thick pink skin rash
under my right arm and breasts which many doctors,
including Naturopathic doctors, personal healing
technique and ointments could not heal. In 2001, one
session with Caroline topped off with the pink ribbon
exercise, uniting my son, husband and me, triggered a
healing within one month! When it returns, I know
my body is telling me the link is broken. I reconnect, use
my ointment and within two days I am rash free.*

~ Lise Couture, Venezuela ~

Enlightening ... elevating ... energizing ...
every experience with Caroline
is an unforgettable experience.

~ s.b. Sudbury, Ontario, Canada ~

I've had the pleasure of briefly meeting with Caroline twice in business settings. The first time I felt a warm feeling towards her. The second time she left me with an understanding of my being I did not know was possible. I found strength, energy and understanding of what life is all about and to be able to accept what LOVE sends my way. I think of her every day since our last meeting and I'm so thankful for the experience we shared. Thank you Caroline and good luck.

~ Linda Miller, Estaire, Ontario, Canada ~

I attended one of Caroline's meetings to get some answers to personal problems. When she insisted I knew a certain technique, I argued with her, totally denying it! She forced me to trust my own instincts regardless of what teachers say and to recognize that I too was both a teacher and a student. Since then, I try to keep my ego in check, allow others to grow at their own speed and try to be the kind of teacher I am always looking for. I realize that even though we all have different styles and methods of doing God's work, what is important is to be the light and to invite others into that blessed circle so they too can understand the Magic of Caroline's famous saying, What would LOVE do? That short meditation has served me well. Merci Caroline!

~ Rev. Gabrielle Lavigne, Garson, Ontario, Canada ~

Every time I see Caroline, our souls connect and our eyes recognize Universal love. I love Caroline because of the love she's shown me, which mirrored the love in me. Tears are in my eyes as I write this, which is the proof that what I say is Truth. Thank you Caroline, for loving me back to health.

~ Susanne Wallner, Ottawa, Ontario, Canada ~

I was coming out of a very dark part of my life - the death of a parent, divorce, alcohol abuse and depression, when I had a reading and then a second one with Caroline. My life definitely took an upward turn. Her vast knowledge and experiences kindled a spark inside me to learn more about my inner self that has grown stronger with time and my own experiences. Her simple, yet very profound, What would LOVE do? has guided me many times when I sought answers to life's difficult questions and dilemmas. Thank you Truth. Thank you Caroline for loving me back to health and for being my friend, you are an angel!

~ Bryan Marino, Brantford, Ontario, Canada ~

What a special friend this gifted lady is! Even when very busy, Caroline takes the time to just listen or help you see why things are happening as they are in your life. She is compassionate, kind, understanding, humble, perceptive, and brimming with love! I wish to return the words she wrote to me, "You personally touched me on my journey in your own very special way.

~ Fern Rancourt, British Columbia, Canada ~

I gave my mom a pink ribbon. My mom rarely tells me she loves me unless I tell her first. After I gave her the ribbon I called her. I didn't mention the ribbon and at the end of our conversation she said, "I love you." Thank you Caroline. You've helped me see life in a different way and for that I am truly grateful.

~ D.S. Kingston, Ontario, Canada ~

It is impossible to write a short sweet testimony about Caroline! I could write a book about how she touches people … the good she does. Caroline taught me to ask, "What would LOVE do?" whenever I have worries or fears. I always get my answer. Visualizing our group holding hands and singing the Sufi Chant calms me and gives me the faith I need to accomplish anything. I can't wait to read her book and the others I know are coming!

~ Carmen Poulin, Conestoga, Ontario, Canada ~

What Would LOVE Do? has been such a gift to my daughter and me. There are times we don't know how to explain, to our sweet kids, the things that go on in and around our lives and using Caroline's Firefly Flight Book, as a fun time together, has helped us find a way to communicate on a level of love and understanding for ourselves, our family and the world around us! Thank you Caroline!

~ Margit Herburger, www.LifeIsValuable.com

Caroline and I met at a friend's birthday party. I had one of my bad headaches and accepted Caroline's offer. She put her hands on my head and my headache went away. It didn't come back for at least a month and just the thought of her hands on my head took the pain away again, just as she said it would. I hardly get headaches now and I now know how to get rid of them.

~ Mirielle Beaudoin, Sturgeon Falls, Ontario, Canada ~

Poem on Back of the FIREFLY FLIGHT BOOK

The Higher Self of Caroline has done a thing so rare,
A brand new way of growing up
for children everywhere.

Drawings and instructions, simple yet profound,
Educate and stimulate each Glow Worm that's around.

How to be a Firefly, surround yourself with light,
You'll fill with love and harmony
upon this magic flight.

Such fun and good vibrations,
your self-expression grows,
A beam of love, a beam of Light,
protect you as you go.

As you fly, you'll energize
with positive direction,
As you fly, you'll soon know why
You've made this great connection.

~ Barry Dale ~ Kingston, Ontario, Canada
Writer, producer, creator and star of
Harrigan the award winning nationally syndicated children's television

There are only two ways
to live your life.
One is as though nothing is a miracle.
The other is as though
everything is a miracle.

~ Albert Einstein ~
https://www.nobelprize.org/nobel_prizes/physics/laureates/1921/einstein-bio.html

WHAT THE COLORS MEAN

Every color of the rainbow has a function. You have colors around and in you that the physical eyes do not see. Isn't it amazing that human eyes were not able to see the color blue in the past, because the eyes were not evolved enough to do so.

There are colors around us that we are unable to see, yet they still affect us. It is common for people to get their colors done now and to use certain colors in prisons and hospitals to influence the way people act.

It has been scientifically and medically researched for many years but few know that your aura, the energy field that surrounds you and is inside you, has many colors and each color reveals a great deal about you.

Your aura changes with your thoughts and the feelings you are experiencing. There are people who can see auras and there are cameras that can take pictures of them. That is called Kirlian photography created by a Russian couple in 1939. Search the Internet for Kirlian photography to learn how to make your own camera and take photos of auras.

What does your color mean? We will look at the rainbow colors and give you a description of their basic functions when bright or dull and your spiritual purpose if the color is dominant in your aura.

RED ... Signifies Energy, the vital life force in the body.

Clear and Bright ... Signifies one who has a strong presence, one who faces fears, and is closely connected to the earth.

Dull or Murky ... Signifies someone who is angry, dealing with fear, survival, and "Who am I?" issues. One can have bowel, lower body and lower back problems.

Spiritual Purpose ... When you have red as your main color in your aura you can energize people just by walking into a room. You can help them work through their fears to help them feel strong and secure. You will often attract people filled with fear and survival issues.

ORANGE ... Signifies Creative, social, sexual energies.

Clear and Bright ... Signifies one who is creative, likes to experience new things, gets along with people and is comfortable with his or her sexual energies. Often a teacher.

Dull and Murky ... Signifies someone who is having difficulty being spontaneous or creative, and is uncomfortable with other people. This one can have problems with his or her sexual organs and large intestines.

Spiritual Purpose ... When you have orange as your main color you are a teacher by example, spontaneous and easy to get along with.

You will often attract people who are awkward around others but comfortable with you. You will often be teaching outside the classroom.

YELLOW ... Signifies the lower mind and emotions.

Clear and Bright ... Signifies a good thinker, one able to think on his or her feet, one who studies well and is comfortable expressing his or her emotions.

Dull and Murky ... Signifies a confused mind, sometimes struggling with understanding the most basic things including expressing his or her emotions. This one may get ulcers, or have problems with his or her digestion, gallbladder, liver, and spleen as a result.

Spiritual Purpose ... When yellow is the main color of your aura, you are to help others understand the workings of their mind, why people do what they do, while expanding your own mind and displaying your emotions and sometimes that of others. This one may be clairsentient (one who knows things through the senses)

GREEN ... Signifies the connection one has with nature and others.

Clear and Bright ... Signifies one that has a great LOVE for nature, people and animals.

Dull and Murky ... Signifies one who can LOVE only those close to him or her and one who is disconnected from nature and one's own heart. This one may experience heart or lung problems.

Spiritual Purpose ... When you have green as the main color in your aura you will have a great LOVE for humanity, the earth and all who live on her. That LOVE moves you to want what is best for all.

Many become nurses, doctors, or work in alternative healing. This one may also have the natural ability to do physical hands-on healings.

BLUE ... Signifies Communication and spiritual healing.

Clear and Bright ... Signifies one that is a good communicator, charismatic.

Dull and Murky ... Signifies one who regrets the words he or she has or has not spoken and will often feel like a victim crying, 'poor me.' When murky this one may experience throat, thyroid, teeth, ear or neck problems.

Spiritual Purpose ... When blue is the main color in your aura you are to speak the truth, to realize the power of your words and to uplift and inspire others with them. This one may also have the power of the spoken word, speak in tongues or be clairaudient (hearing thoughts,

INDIGO ... Signifies the ability to receive inspiration, to manifest things.

Clear and Bright ... Signifies one who can be inspired, is very positive and has a good imagination.

Dull and Murky ... Signifies one who is narrow minded, a negative thinker and lacking imagination.

This one may have problems with his or her eyes, headaches, or hair loss.

Spiritual Purpose ... When indigo is the main color in your aura you will be inventive, inspired and you will inspire others. This one may also be clairvoyant (sees angels, auras, people's thoughts).

VIOLET ... Signifies the bigger picture, transforming energies.

Clear and Bright ... Signifies one who can change energy from negative to positive. This person has had awakenings, can get lost in space and time, sees the bigger picture and does not get affected by the chaos around him or her.

Dull and Murky ... Signifies one who cannot expand his or her consciousness, feels stuck in his or her situation, unable to change. This one can be depressed even suicidal.

Spiritual Purpose ... When indigo is the main color in your aura don't be surprised to find yourself in the middle of chaos, drama, negative situations; not because you deserve it but because you are a transformer of energy. You are that blue/ violet part of the flame (the hottest part) that changes ice into water, fear into courage, slow moving negative energy into faster moving positive energy. You are here to show people how to be on this earth but not of it. This one may be the mystic, guru, the master in the poor man's clothing.

WHITE ... Signifies the totality of all colors, purity, and oneness with all.

Clear and Bright ... Signifies high spiritual energy, a very evolved soul, often seen as a 'halo' in pictures of the holy ones.

A Little Dull ... Signifies one with a great deal of potential to be a master.

Spiritual Purpose ... You are to be the Master, to be

LOVE in action. "You can do the same as me and even more."

Great humility fills one who has either evolved to that level or simply remembers the truth about being a true spiritual being having a human experience.

Additional colors that may be in your aura:

GOLD ... Signifies the higher mind, the philosopher, one who can understand abstract thinking, universal mind.

Spiritual Purpose ... You are to teach by example and to either explain the unexplainable or bring new teachings to all. The downside to having such an evolved mind is not having many to share your thoughts with who can understand what you are talking about.

PINK ... Signifies universal LOVE. One who can LOVE all unconditionally. Seldom dull. It may be a lighter pink which shows one's potential to LOVE all.

Spiritual Purpose … To be LOVE in action. You will be the earth mother, loving and nurturing all. An unusual thing happens when you are this much LOVE. Some interpret this LOVE as sexual and find themselves falling in LOVE with you. When that happens, simply speak and walk the truth.

Asking, "What would LOVE do?" will give you the perfect thing to say or do to help you through these possibly uncomfortable moments.

Storms
make trees take deeper roots.

~ Dolly Parton ~
http://www.imdb.com/name/nm0000573/bio

GLOSSARY

Because *What Would LOVE Do?* is a title that would catch the attention of many who are not familiar with metaphysical terminology, definitions have been kept simple to avoid confusion. The following is an explanation of some of the words and names used that might be new you and websites where you can find more information.

AURA … Energy field surrounding a person or thing able to be seen by some. Can be photographed with Kirlian photography. The aura changes with thoughts, emotions, pain, drug usage, and the influence of others. http:// skepdic.com/auras.html

Visit this site for a fun way to find out what your colour is in your aura.

http://www.testcafe.com/color/color.html

Remember these are just a few of the colours that exist in and around our bodies. You have more than one color in your aura or energy field. Also remember that someone else's aura will be seen through your own, so that must be considered. Always remember it is good to read or listen to what others say about colours, or dream analysis however, your own 'gut' feeling is always the best judge.

BHAGAVAN SRI SATHYA SAI BABA … *I have come to light the lamp of LOVE, to see that it shines with added luster.*

I have not come on behalf of any religion, I have come to tell you of this unitary faith, this spiritual principle, this path of LOVE.

http://www.sathyasai.org/

BREATHARIANS … Claim to live on prana alone. By periodically meditating instead of eating and drinking, they are able to be sustained from the ethers.

http://www.scona.net.au/~hubbca/breatharian-ism.htm

CHAKRAS … Centres of energy within the body that spiral and draw energy from the universe to feed the body. When going in a reverse spin the energy is drawn from the body outwards, draining it. There are hundreds of charkas in the body but the seven major ones each has its own colour, sound, psychological influence on the body and psychic/ spiritual ability (gifts of the holy spirit). When energy moves through the charkas a physical reaction is experienced by the body. Example-when the heart chakra is becoming larger many feel they are having a heart attack.

http://www.llewellynencyclopedia.com/article.php?id=249

CLAIRSENTIENT … Experiencing other realities or entities through one or more of the five senses.

http://www.crystalinks.com/clairs.html

INTEGRATED AWARENESS TECHNIQUE … Now the Perceptive Awareness Technique. "The answers are within you.

Perceptive Awareness Training is the key that unlocks the door, lifts the veil, the roadblocks, the insecurities that keep us from realizing our dreams."

http://www.perceptiveawareness.com/main.htm

KIRLIAN PHOTOGRAPHY ... In 1939, Semyon Kirlian discovered by accident that if an object on a photographic plate is subjected to a high-voltage

electric field, an image is created on the plate. The image looks like a colored halo or coronal discharge. This image is said to be a physical manifestation of the spiritual aura or "life force" which allegedly surrounds each living thing.

http://skepdic.com/kirlian.html

MARIEL HEALING ... In a MariEl session the practitioners channel the energy, which is very loving and gentle, the same way Reiki is channeled either hands on or with the hands not touching the body, but close.

METAPHYSICS ... A branch of philosophy concerned with the nature of ultimate reality.

http://encarta.msn.com/encnet/refpages/RefArticle.aspx?refid= 7615553

PARAMAHANSA YOGANANDA ... recognized as a world teacher, an enlightened exponent of the universal Science of Yoga, a benefactor of mankind. His nature was universal, his life a blend of the spiritual wisdom of his motherland and the practical efficiency of his adopted country.

In his Autobiography of a Yogi he gives us an account of a singular search for truth, skillfully interwoven with scientific explanations of the subtle but definite laws by which yogis perform miracles and attain self-mastery. He describes his training in India under Swami Shri Yukteswar Giri.

http://users.pandora.be/ananda/ygnd.htm

PRANA ... Is the all-pervading vital energy of the universe, according to Hinduism. It is the Indian version of chi.

http://skepdic.com/prana.html

PSYCHOMETRY ... The ability or faculty to perceive the characters, surroundings, and events connected with a person by holding an object belonging to that person in one's hands.

http://www.themystica.com/mystica/articles/p/psychometry.html

REIKI ... A healing technique which enables the facilitator to access, deliver and co-create energy dependent upon the level of the facilitator.

http://www.reikisecrets.com/faq.htm

RUNES ... Ancient stones with symbols on them. Each having their own meaning.

http://www.stemnet.nf.ca/CITE/v_runes.htm

SHIRLEY MACLAINE ... *I think we all choose the paths of our lives. I knew I wanted to be a 'communicator' from the very beginning.*

So, I communicated through fifty (50) films, many TV and stage shows and nine books.

http://www.shirleymaclaine.com/bio.html

TERESA NEUMANN ... 1898-1962 Teresa Neumann's life changed radically after her miraculous recovery from paralysis and total blindness at the age of 25. A year later, she received the stigmata and began fasting, which lasted 36 years until her death.

Her only nourishment was the Holy Eucharist and for this reason the Nazi authorities, during World War II, withdrew her food rationing card and gave her a double rationing of soap to wash her towels and clothing, because every Friday she would be drenched in Blood while she was in ecstasy, experiencing the Passion of Christ.

Hitler was very fearful of Teresa. Teresa Neumann was born in Konnersreuth Germany, on April 8th, 1898 from an extremely poor Catholic family. Her greatest ambition was to become a missionary in Africa but that was not possible as she was a victim of an accident at the age of 20 when a horrible fire broke out in a nearby plant and Teresa went to help and in the process of passing buckets of water to stop the flames, she got a horrible lesion in her spinal cord that caused a paralysis in both her legs and complete blindness.

Teresa then passed her days in prayer. One day her miraculous recovery occurred in the presence of Father Naber who wrote:

"Teresa described a vision of a great light and an extraordinary, sweet voice that was asking her if she wished to be healed.

Teresa gave the most surprising answer when she replied that to her it would not make any difference whether she would be healed, stay the way she was or even die, as long as it was the will of God.

The mysterious voice told her that 'that very day she would receive a small joy; the healing of her infirmities, however that she would still have a lot of suffering to endure in her future.

For a while, Teresa lived in good health, however, in 1926 her most important mystical experiences started and lasted until the day she died. She received the stigmata, and she began a complete fasting, with the Eucharist as her only nourishment.

Father Naber, who administered Communion to Teresa every day, wrote: "In her, God's promised word is accomplished: 'My Flesh is real food and my Blood is a true drink'". Teresa offered the Lord her physical suffering - due to the loss of blood caused by the stigmata that started every Thursday during the day when Jesus' Passion started, until Sunday, His Resurrection. This suffering was offered, through her intercession, for sinners that asked for help.

Every time she would be called to a person's death bed, she would be witness to that soul's judgment, as it is usual to happen right after death.

http://ww.mysticssofthechurch.com/2009/12/therese-neumann-mysticvictim0-soul.html

Creativity is intelligence having fun!

~ Albert Einstein ~
https://www.nobelprize.org/nobel_prizes/physics/laureates/1921/einstein-bio.html

MORE OF CAROLINE'S CREATIONS

The Firefly Flight Book

A Metaphysical Workbook for Kids Aged 2 to 200
A one-week intensive, yet simple to understand workshop covering angels,
death, healing, blessings, thoughts, sound, how to deal with anger, fear,
and more.
eBook, Hardcopy and Kindle

Love's Magical Connection

Heals the Pain of Separation
Caused by Death ~ Divorce ~ Distance ~ Duty ~ Drama
Original Story ... For Military ... For Pet Lovers
eBook, Hardcopy and Kindle

To Be Or Not To Be ~ Stop Suicide's Seduction

An inspired poem used by
counselors, ministers, mental health workers, and parents.
eBook, Booklet and Kindle

As You Think ~ So It Is

Seven Universal Laws ~ Change Your Way of Being
Simple, profound, inspired during the Gulf War and is applicable today.
eBook, Booklet and Kindle

I Am A Hologram of God

This totally changed how I see and live my life!
~ Robert S., Timmons, Ontario, Canada ~
eBook, Booklet and Kindle

The ABCs of Spirituality ~ 101

Awaken Be Co-Create
200 pages of teachings and exercises
eBook, Booklet and Kindle

Dolphin Whispers

They teach us what we need not what we want.
eBook, Booklet, Kindle

Magical Mystical Memories - CD

Short Stories That Have Triggered Spontaneous Healings
*Your voice and stories put me in an altered state.
I don't have any more pain!*

~ Janice B. Sudbury, Ontario, Canada ~

ARTICLES TOO NUMEROUS TO MENTION

CONTACT

Caroline would LOVE to hear from you.
Invite her to be a guest speaker, to lead workshops,
to do home shows, personal consultations
or to lead retreats
FOR ALL AGES!

POSTAL ADDRESS
Caroline McIntosh,
94 Alma, Hanmer, Ontario, Canada P3P 1R2

LET'S TALK
705-831-2022

EMAIL
Love@IAmCaroline.com
or
WhatWouldLoveDo@Eastlink.ca

VISIT
www.IAmCaroline.com
FOR A FREE GIFT ON WELCOME PAGE
And
www.WhatWouldLOVEDo.online

LET'S BE FACEBOOK FRIENDS
www.Facebook.com/1stCarolineMcIntosh

LET'S SKYPE
Loves1stCaroline

*Educating the mind
without educating the heart
is no education at all.*

~ Aristotle ~
https://www.biography.com/people/aristotle-9188415

COMMENTS, QUESTIONS OR TESTIMONIAL FOR WWLD?

What was the overall message I got out of this book?

_____

_____

_____

_____

_____

_____

_____

_____

_____

_____

_____

_____

_____

_____

I Am God.
You are God.
The only difference is
I know it.

~ Sri Sathya Sai Baba ~
https://en.wikipedia.org/wiki/Sathya_Sai_Baba

MY PERSONAL STORY
For Possible Inclusion in Vol II of WWLD?

_____

_____

_____

_____

_____

_____

_____

_____

_____

_____

_____

_____

_____

_____

_____

And I'd choose you;

In a hundred lifetimes,

In a hundred worlds,

In any version of reality,

I'd find you and

I'd choose you.

~ The Chaos of Stars ~